The True Story of Murphy Ranch

Nazi Nonsense in Los Angeles

Stanton K. Stevens

DEDICATION

Dedicated to my grandfather and teacher, Norman F. Stevens.

CONTENTS

ACKNOWLEDGMENTS

I want to acknowledge the many people who helped this book come to be; my incredibly patient, supportive, and perceptive wife Valerie, my father Carlile (Steve) Stevens, uncle Robin Stevens, aunt Theanne (Toni) Pepper, brother Todd Stevens, cousins Carolyn, Chris, David, Marcie, and all the others who helped. And Randy Young; you and I may never tell quite the same story but thank you so much for putting the quest for truth above all else, and for the wonderful images and information you have provided.

INTRODUCTION

Living memories of the 1930s are almost gone. Only people in their nineties and older remember the decade firsthand. The time between the world wars was very different from now. Great ideological battles simmered, fueled by extreme poverty in the Great Depression. Unions battled the capitalists, communists and socialists fought for their unreachable ideals, and fascism and militarism quickly moved to dominate, promising order in the chaos. There was widespread anticipation of big changes to come and fear of how those changes would happen. The fear turned out to be justified.

My grandparents were raising their young children in Pasadena, California as the 1930s unfolded. They were scared, too. But they were different. They had the wealth to act. Perhaps most people in Los Angeles know what they did, but not through the true story. An urban legend about Nazis, with roots in the fear and suspicion of the 1930s, has sprung up about the retreat they built for their family. This book is the first to tell the true story of the Stevens family that built Murphy Ranch, in Rustic Canyon in the Pacific Palisades north of Los Angeles. It will be clear how far the legend wandered from the truth. And, as is often the case, the true story turns out to be more interesting than the legend. This is the story of one of the most fascinating, yet unknown, families in Los Angeles's history, the family of Norman and Winona Stevens. As their grandson, and someone who has always had a special interest in Norman, I feel that it is my job to set the story straight. I have worked closely with Norman and Winona's surviving children to create this book: the real story of the Stevens and Murphy Ranch.

But Murphy Ranch is just one chapter in the unusual one-hundred-year life of Norman Stevens. In the 1960s and 1970s, people began looking for spiritual teachers. If they looked hard enough and were not fooled along the way by the countless self-styled gurus, they found Norman and his second wife Josephine, the authors of the Rainbow Bridge Books. Every culture and place, including California, has its hidden spiritual side, and teachers of what only a few are ready to understand. The teachers are shamans in some cultures, wise men in others, the true Indian gurus/saints, the Tibetan holy men, and the great teachers in every country who seem ordinary and unknown to everyone but the students who desperately need their help in seeing through the illusory, transient belief systems of the times. Norman spent his life seeking the one reality behind these teachings and eventually helping others to know what he had found. So, if this book takes a turn into a world that you have not explored, don't be surprised. And don't be afraid.

Their teachings, like all the esoteric teachings worth anything at all, are about love, brotherhood, the recognition of our real nature, our potential power, and unity. It is my aim to make this book an enjoyable exploration of not only the lives of Norman, Winona, and Josephine Stevens but of what was most important to them and what they were so uniquely able to give to the world. Not to mention, I also show how completely incompatible these people were with Nazi fascism, a movement designed to enslave humanity rather than enlighten and free it.

I will tell more stories from the later phase of Norman's life toward the end of this book. Until recently, I only knew a little about his life before that phase. This book tells that equally remarkable story, the true version, and is intended to replace the surprising and false story that is currently repeated far too often.

There is so much more that I couldn't include in an engaging narrative. If you are interested, I encourage you to visit my website, https://murphyranch.org.

1 FULL CIRCLE

True adventures are rare in my world of high-tech professionals. But I have discovered they are not so rare in my family, and now it was my turn. My grandparents had great wealth and did some surprising things with it. I was to have an adventure exploring the abandoned survival retreat for which my grandparents were called Nazis. It has been an interesting challenge to confront and explore the origins of such a story. When I first heard of the urban legend, I knew I must see the place for myself and bring as much light as possible into the murky tale. My father and uncle had lived there as youths; I arranged for us all to meet in southern California, and now the time had come to visit the place at the heart of the urban legend.

On May 1, 2014, my father, Carlile (Steve) Stevens (he went by Steve most of his life, I will use that name for him in this book), and my uncle, Robin Stevens, joined me to look out over the sunlit coastal California canyon of the old family estate built by my grandparents. They had last seen it in 1949, sixty-five years before. They were celebrities that day. Several park rangers and Los Angeles city officials had helped arrange the opening of the gates of Murphy Ranch for this event; they were with us, very interested in meeting the people who had lived here so long ago. Today the fogs of legend would lift! They looked intently at Steve and Robin and wondered how these people fit into the bizarre stories they had heard about this place. My wife Valerie, brother Todd, and cousin Carolyn (Robin's daughter) were with us, equally curious to hear the stories our fathers would tell.

"I don't know about this," Robin had muttered earlier as we drove up to the meeting place. We were driving to a rendezvous with our family's past, where memories of people long dead, and dreams long forgotten would be revived. I worried that the 80+ year-old brothers would suffer from the experience. But there was also the promise of a re-acquaintance with their youthful selves and the energetic and positive view of life they had in the 1940s. Our family is creative and adaptive, eager to harness the breakthroughs of science and whatever opportunities arise, and usually looks forward to the future. And there was hope that Robin would point his finger at places that would greatly impact all our lives. I will say more about that later.

Original gate from 1930s, torn down 2016   *photo by Valerie Stevens*

The vehicles gathered at the old gates to Murphy Ranch. The original gates from the 1930s still stood, and still prevented vehicles from entering. The masonry walls around them were broken through in places, marked thoroughly with graffiti, and the ironwork gates were misaligned. A Park Ranger came to our driver-side window and said, "Mr. Stevens?" Four men answered. He opened the gates that had been closed to all but the rangers' vehicles for many years. We were allowed to follow the Ranger's truck and the city officials' truck down the decaying, winding road in a 4-wheel drive vehicle we rented. Sector superintendent Stephen Bylin, Ranger Tim Hayden, and some interested city officials joined our caravan.

Not far in from the gate, we got out to look down into the empty ruin of a huge water tank, 60 feet across and 30 feet tall. As we stood at the rim, Robin spoke of swimming in the dark, cool water of the 300,000-plus gallon water tank, under the wooden roof, in the 1940s. He took friends and girlfriends there. Carlile (Steve) also swam there, but only by himself. Now the cement tank was empty and roofless, with rusted ladders clinging to the sides. The interior walls were covered with a psychedelic profusion of many years of graffiti, the bottom with debris and empty spray paint cans. The smell of fresh paint hung in the air, as it did every day we visited. A few months before, a helicopter had been called to the site to lift someone out of the tank who was probably afraid to use the decrepit ladders. Since our visit, the concrete tank has been demolished. Now there is only overgrown scrub where it was. The gates are also gone, torn down with the water tank in February 2016.

The 360,000-gallon tank, 2014, torn down 2016   *photo by Valerie Stevens*

Another view of the tank   *photo by Valerie Stevens*

This tank and another 100,000-gallon tank had been filled from wells and provided water for irrigation, livestock, and dwellings. Self-sufficiency was part of the design of "The Canyon," as the family referred to it. Steve told the rangers about the complex irrigation system and valves, with miles of copper pipe to carry the water to terraced hillsides, where orchards had grown. They might still have grown since they were trees that could withstand dry conditions once established, but the huge Mandeville fire had swept across Murphy Ranch in 1978, and only the biggest trees survived.

The second water tank.   *Photo by Valerie Stevens*

The road down into the ranch.   *Photo by Stanton Stevens*

Everyone was talking at once, Robin and Steve each telling stories of the ranch to the rangers and officials. The rangers especially seemed happy to hear a new story, rather than the one that had always had the flavor of an unlikely exaggeration, especially as it changed and enlarged over the years.

But it was the only story they knew, and they told it to us as they had told it to visitors for the last 20 years. They could hear how it rang false and were embarrassed to be telling it to the ones it had slandered.

Back in the vehicles, we continued winding slowly into the canyon, down the asphalt road built in the 1930s, dodging large holes. The trees around us were larger as we progressed, shading us at times from the sun in the 90+ degree heat. On our left was the house in which Conrad Anderson had lived. Not much was left but chunks of the collapsed structure, with a tree growing through the remains of a washing machine. But for Steve and Robin, there were unsettling memories of Anderson, the man who had saved Robin's life, yet nearly ruined the family. Whatever was not right about Murphy Ranch probably originated with Anderson, a charismatic, powerful, and evil person. I will tell you more about him in Chapter 6.

They looked for a second house at the bottom of the canyon, a twin to the first, but there was no trace of it. We learned later that it had been moved off the property in one piece.

The building that had housed the generators stood, and still stands today, solid and empty, otherwise nearly unchanged, except for the graffiti completely covering the 8-inch-thick concrete walls, inside and out. Now it was a temple for art that was immediately painted over by the next graffiti artist. Most of it rarely lasted more than a few days. Some of it was good, including an angelic figure we saw that day. But a day later even that was mostly painted over by another team of "artists." The two big diesel-powered generators were long gone. But Steve pointed out exactly where they had been, and where everything else had been in the building. His responsibility as a child of 11 was to keep the generators running. He had often slept in the noisy building, ready to jump up and start the second generator if the first one started sputtering. It took all his body weight to spin the wheel which helped start the generator.

The Power House, 2014.   *Photo: Valerie Stevens*

Inside the Power House   *Photo: Valerie Stevens*

Behind the Power House stood the 30,000-gallon fuel oil tank that had supplied the generators. It was crumpled as if a giant fist had punched it. Most likely it had filled with steam or fuel vapors during the fire that swept through in 1978, then collapsed later from external pressure when the gases inside condensed to create a vacuum. Norman told me years ago about an additional tank with thousands of gallons of lubricating oil buried near the

Power House, it may not have been discovered yet. As we looked at all this together, I shared my cousin Carolyn's sense of wonder at the scale of our grandparents' creation and the determination they must have had to build such a place. She was particularly sad their great dream had come to this.

A pipe stuck out of the ground; it had graffiti on it. A curb along a path was a swath of rainbow letters. Seemingly inaccessible points inside and outside the Power House had been made into canvases by artists who must have brought ladders with them. None of this was legal, of course, but the property is owned by the City of Los Angeles, technically not in the jurisdiction of the rangers of the nearby parks and forests. There has been a long-running controversy about who should police it, who should take responsibility for safety hazards, and who should determine the fate of the ruins. There was even some question as to whether to preserve the ruins due to the Nazi legend. But my father's and uncle's testimony to the real story probably helped them in their decision. In February 2016 the city finally stepped in. They demolished the big water tank, the front gate, and the ruins of the main house. They also boarded up the Power House. Maybe the art inside is now a frozen snapshot of the ever-changing surfaces that went before. It depends on how well they boarded up the building, I doubt they can stop the determined young artists.

The tank behind the Power House.   *Photo: Valerie Stevens*

Graffiti angels   *Photo: Valerie Stevens*

The ruins of the main house, 2014, removed 2016   *Photo: Valerie Stevens*

We went on down the road to discover that what had been the main house was now a twisted pile of rusty metal with only one vertical wall. It was no ordinary structure; the walls had been made of steel, now collapsing in sheets. The arches over the road remained. Robin looked over the slope running from the first arch to the creek but didn't see the big honeysuckle bush he remembered. Sixty-five years is a long time. This twisted wreckage was the saddest sight of the day. The family and others had lived in this house. The building was part of a larger plan for a huge mansion complex and was originally to be a garage. But it was redesigned to house the family when the war approached, and it became clear the larger plan would not be feasible in time.

Valerie, Stanton, Carlile, Robin, and Todd Stevens May 1, 2014.   *Photo: Todd Stevens*

Carlile (Steve) and Robin Stevens   *Photo: Valerie Stevens*

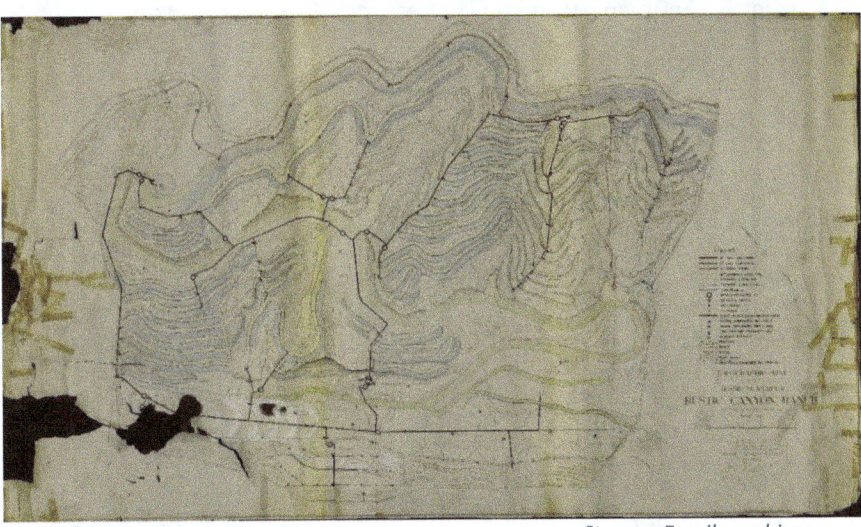

Map of the ranch   *Stevens Family archives*

The canyons around Los Angeles are dry, so Robin and Steve were surprised to see large trees and heavy vegetation all along the bottom of the canyon, it was quite different than when they had last seen it all in 1949. They remembered wide, clear grounds, with enclosures for farm animals like cows, chickens, rabbits, and ducks. Three acres were planted with alfalfa. There was a mule named Gabriel and a bull named Gulliver. There were beehives, and thousands of olive, lemon, orange, grapefruit, apricot, pear, apple, avocado, peach, pomegranate, plum, carob, and fig trees on the terraced hillsides. Nine long concrete staircases dropped down the sides of the canyon to maintain the terraces; the longest staircase was over five hundred steps, the others nearly as long. They were well built, nearly unchanged today, a marvel to hikers. I can tell you that going the length of a five-hundred-step staircase is a serious exercise, up or down. On my last visit in 2023, we saw a black rattlesnake coiled next to the stairs.

Robin and Steve told everyone stories about life on the ranch. The fascinated rangers asked many questions. Hikers came through, some with their own tales of Murphy Ranch. One fellow reported meeting Tom Hanks walking through, his home was in the "Capri" neighborhood we had walked through the other day to get to the ranch. Another said she had hiked most of the way in with some friends, only to be frightened and turn around to leave quickly. They had seen ahead of them someone near the ruins playing German marching music and goose-stepping in uniform!

We gathered the family, rangers, and officials, for a few photos taken by two young women who were hiking through. Most of us will never see Murphy Ranch again. And now the ruins behind the photos they took are gone, even that moment of the recent past feels like part of another era.

2 NAZIS? YOU'RE KIDDING, RIGHT?

In March 2013, my father Carlile (Steve) Stevens mentioned something to me about how upset my uncle Robin Stevens was about the Nazi rumors in Los Angeles; some ridiculous story they had heard about "The Canyon," which was what they had called Murphy Ranch while growing up there. The story was that Nazis had met and marched there, been arrested there, and the place had been built for them. It even said the owners of the property, my grandparents, Norman and Winona Stevens, had been Nazi sympathizers!

This was obvious nonsense, and I was very surprised such stories were being told. I knew my grandfather well. I had searched for my grandparents' names on the internet over the years and found almost nothing, just an article about Winona Stevens selling a collection of the letters of British reformer Richard Carlile to the Huntington Library in Pasadena. It turns out the published Nazi legend stories misspelled their names "Stephens." Once I knew what to look for, I found stories online going back to 1990, with names like Nazi Outpost: Rustic Canyon, Hitler Bunker in Los Angeles, and Murphy Ranch, Nazi Enclave, etc. It was not just internet blogs, there were articles in the Los Angeles Times. I was shocked to find nearly everyone I knew from Los Angeles had heard about Murphy Ranch and the supposed Nazis, both from these stories and by word of mouth. A mysterious "Herr Schmidt" supposedly convinced my grandparents to build the place. Robin had heard about a Los Angeles Times story at some point in the 90s and was angry about it, but when a lawyer told him it was too late to sue or force a retraction, he decided to just let it go. After all, how long could such a crazy story last? That turned out to be a mistake. There is even a Wikipedia page dedicated to the story now, presenting it as factual! I wish Robin had nipped it in the bud back then by contacting the main source of the story, Randy Young. All the recent newspaper, online, and TV stories trace back to him and his mother, Betty Lou Young, starting with her 1975 book Rustic Canyon and the Story of the Uplifters. Later I will dig into the roots and growth of the urban legend.

Before I say anything else about the stories and Randy Young, I want to point out that he is now telling a different story and was very happy to work with my family on getting to the bottom of the tale. He has shared everything he knows about the story with us, has met Robin and Carlile, and promised to stop associating our family with Nazis. He is serious about being accurate as a historian. He is as dismayed as we are at the exaggerations added to the story as the years have gone by. It was quite a moment for him to meet the descendants of the people about whom he had been telling Nazi stories for 40 years. And that is also a story for another chapter.

It is time for the Nazi nonsense story to end. It is an insult to the people in my family, residents of Murphy Ranch during World War II, who fought and worked to help the United States win the war. To see such a flimsy fantasy take root to the point where it is unquestioned, at the expense of my family's true story, is an example of ignorance overcoming facts, gossip overriding history. I will give more details later, but to summarize: Norman Stevens worked at Douglas Aircraft during the war, as head of quality control for fighter planes. His oldest son Dale Stevens, who lived at Murphy Ranch, earned a purple heart fighting Nazis in Europe, with General Patton's army. Dale's younger brother Robin brought supplies to US troops in Japan, as a member of the militarized Merchant Marine.

When evil gangs like the Nazi leaders or the Japanese militarists try to conquer and enslave humanity, good people stand up and fight, and my family worked and fought for good. The Nazis were humorless products of national psychosis. They embodied the destructive extremes of nationalism and racism. Brainwashed from youth to be willing martyrs for their truly evil leadership, and trained to be heartless murderers for that cause, the party members and German soldiers were an example of the worst possibilities of humanity. It is hard to find a conflict, before or since World War II, with such a sharp line between good and evil. This distinction was obvious to my grandfather, Norman Stevens. As a spiritual teacher and author, he taught in his later life about the importance of love, brotherhood, compassion, and right action. It is laughable to think he could ever have been a "Nazi sympathizer," but it is slander, nonetheless. This book is intended to clear Norman's and our family's name.

Let me tell you the story of the real Norman and Winona Stevens, their family, and the surprising actual history of Murphy Ranch.

3 A SUDDEN FORTUNE

In the last year of World War I, Norman Ferdinand Stevens of Lewiston, Maine, had a stroke of good fortune. He dropped out of his undergraduate studies at MIT to enlist in the "United States Army Air Service Balloon Corps". His unit was sent to Europe, where they were all killed, just like the unit before them, and just as he would have been. Instead, Norman was sent to California to train others. This was quite a new place for someone who grew up as the son of Ferdinand E. Stevens, Sheriff of Androscoggin County, Maine. Ferd was a dynamic and colorful character, you can read more about him here: https://murphyranch.org. Norman's years working in Boston and studying Engineering and Physics at MIT had not prepared him for what Los Angeles had in store.

Los Angeles, California in 1918 was poised to grow and shine in ways no one could imagine. The motion picture industry was just getting started, but Southern California had already become known as a kind of paradise. It had attracted a variety of people, including a lovely young woman and her wealthy mother: Winona and Theophila Campbell Bassett. Theophila traced her ancestry back to the Mayflower and was proud of her grandfather Richard Carlile, the English reformer. Her daughter Winona named her third son Carlile. Theophila's mother was named Theophila, too! When she was asked if a granddaughter should also have the name, she said "Heavens no, anything but that!" Her youngest grandchild was then named Norma Theanne.

The Bassetts moved from Chicago to Pasadena, California in the early 1900s. They traveled back and forth to Chicago at first. The two women drove from Pasadena to the East Coast in about 1914, quite a feat at the time. It was even written up in newspapers along the route. Winona liked to tell the story of driving across California and seeing a road sign that said "Needles, 99 miles." Several miles later they saw a sign that said the same thing, "Needles, 99 miles." Miles later, they were relieved to see a sign, "Needles, 98 miles." Miles after that was another sign: "Needles, 99 miles."

Winona rode a horse in the Rose Parade of 1910 when she was 18. She left Pasadena for four years to attend Stanford University, class of 1914, a member of the Pi Beta Phi sorority. It is possible to find playbills online for the plays she acted in, such as her role as "Mehitable Mooney" in a play called *The Girl and the Voice*, by Paul Eliel, a junior opera. She graduated with a degree in Economics and moved back to Pasadena with her mother. She remained connected with her sorority sisters over the years. Mother and daughter were socialites, supporting the growing cultural scene in Pasadena. Theophila donated money to help build the Pasadena Playhouse. Winona helped found Delta Phi Epsilon, a nationwide service organization dedicated to kindergarten in 1925.

Norman met Winona at a dance set up for military personnel in Pasadena. He was good-looking and serious, and the military uniform suited his straight back. Winona told others years later that one reason that she noticed him was that he had the only clean handkerchief. He must have offered it to her for some reason. His years at MIT may also have impressed her, and Norman may have been impressed with Winona's degree, but the chemistry of two attractive young people was certain to be a factor. This chemistry was continually under the watchful eye of Winona's mother, Theophila. When Norman brought flowers to Winona, he always had to bring some for Theophila, too. She chaperoned everything they did together. Theophila did not let Winona get far from her at any time; when Winona went to Stanford, Theophila got herself appointed house mother at Winona's sorority. Nevertheless, the courtship proceeded smoothly, and soon Norman and Winona were engaged.

Where Norman met Winona   *Stevens Family Archives*

Two weeks before their wedding date, Winona said, "I want to tell you something." Norman had the quick thought that she was engaged to someone else, and said, "You don't have to tell me anything." Winona told him she had $300,000 in the bank and had inherited twenty million dollars. And there was more money still to come. Twenty million 1920 dollars is comparable to over a billion 2022 dollars in economic clout. In Norman's family, $1000 was a fortune. He had no idea how it would affect his life, but he was about to marry into one of the wealthiest families in the country and share in the Bassett fortune.

Norman and Winona Stevens, wedding day, March 13, 1920   *Stevens Family Archives*

Arthur Judson Bassett, Winona's father, built his fortune in Chicago, as a partner in Grand Crossing Tack and Nail Works. He and his partners, the Hutchison brothers, invented an efficient process for the creation of wire nails, what we think of now as ordinary round shaft nails. Their business grew quickly, and they were in the right place. Chicago in 1900 was a hub of the growing steel industry. When they had problems with a union that cut them off from all their steel suppliers, they bought their own steel mill. When the unions retaliated by cutting them off from the mines, they bought their own mine. Their business grew steadily until they were eventually acquired by Republic Steel after Arthur's death. Arthur died in 1902, at age 50.

Alfred Hutchison and Arthur J Basset   *Stevens Family Archives*

Grand Crossing Tack and Nail Works – Chicago   *Stevens Family Archives*

Diagram of the steel mill from the Republic Reporter, 1980.

The story of what happened to the vast wealth he left for Theophila and his only surviving child, Winona, is a long and interesting one. The money Norman and Winona spent to develop the property called Murphy Ranch was only a small fraction of the inheritance. Where the rest of the money went is the subject of Chapter 7, "Losing a Large Fortune."

After Norman and Winona married on March 13, 1920, they lived in Norman's house. It was a comfortable home in Pasadena that Norman had bought with the money he had earned in his job, designing a refinery for a local oil company. He was a good engineer, even before he attended MIT he had designed and built his own glider and airplane. When Winona had first told him about the $300,000, his reply was, "You don't need it. I have a good job and I have lots of money, so I can give you anything you need. You can just take it and store it away." He had a lot to learn about wealthy people, and what it meant to live as one of them.

Norman and his glider.   *Stevens Family Archives*

Norman and his airplane.   *Stevens Family Archives*

Wedding night selfie of Norman and Winona.   *Stevens Family Archives*

After they had only been married a short time, Norman found that this wealth was everywhere around him. When Winona told him Theophila had bought the house across the street from them, Norman thought, "Fine, now I don't have to buy a house (for Theophila), ok." Then things began to be delivered over there, fancy furniture, etc. When a grand piano was delivered, he gave up. He asked Winona, "Would you like to move across the street? You've made a groove in the pavement going back and forth." Her reply: "Oh yes, I would love that!" They sold his house, moved across the street, and he was living in his mother-in-law's house.

1875 La Loma Road, Pasadena   *Stevens Family Archives*

Now they lived as wealthy people did at the time, in a large house with servants. Their house at 875 La Loma Road in Pasadena is still there, and at the time it was one of the nicest houses in Pasadena. It is currently valued at over seven million dollars. Another couple moved in with them too, at Theophila's invitation, and all were Christian Scientists. There was some competition as to which of the wives would have the first baby. Winona's and Priscilla's babies were born not far apart. All six of Norman and Winona's children were born there:

Colin, born 1923, died as an infant
Dale Bassett Stevens, born 1925, died 1996
Robin Campbell Stevens, born 1927, died 2019
David, born 1929, died as an infant
Carlile Richmond Stevens, born 1931, died 2023
Norma Theanne Stevens, born 1932

I can't imagine the suffering of this young couple losing their baby. Reading the birth announcement and then seeing no further mention of Colin in the press only hints at the void he must have left. They went through it again six years later. Norman never spoke of these lost babies to me, but the experiences must have helped make him the stoic, sober person he was.

Norman with Robin, Dale, and baby Carlile.   *Stevens Family Archives*

Theophila was an energetic woman, very active in the WCTU – Women's Christian Temperance Union. This organization was primarily anti-alcohol. She traveled to Europe often, sometimes with Winona. She loved Los Angeles and was a booster for it when abroad. My favorite story about that is from one of her visits to Italy. She and other wealthy society people were sitting on a veranda on a warm evening in Sorrento, or somewhere else near Mt. Vesuvius. The volcano was erupting, with visible lava, and one of the

Italian men said, "I'm sure you don't have anything like that in Los Angeles!"

"Oh, the Los Angeles fire department would put that out in a minute!" was her reply.

In the 1930s, Theophila began to have some problems due to her age, and at one point thought of her first grandchild as her child. Later, her wealth attracted a young stranger who persuaded her he was a long-lost nephew, causing more problems. The family moved her to a very nice house in Hermosa Beach, where she was taken care of by hired help. Not long after Theanne was born in 1932, the rest of the family moved to a house they built that year on Bellevue Avenue, keeping the La Loma house for parties. The whole family moved to Theophila's house in Hermosa Beach in 1934 or 1935 when Theophila's health became worse. Theophila bought every lot between her house and the beach to preserve the view. Theophila died November 22, 1937.

275 W Bellevue Dr., Pasadena   *Stevens Family Archives*

2045 Monterey Boulevard, Hermosa Beach, CA   *Stevens Family Archives*

The kids report that the best times of their childhood were while living in the Hermosa Beach house. There are old 16 mm movies of the kids playing in the sea there.

Shirley Temple was the number one box office draw for Hollywood from 1935 – 1938 and lived nearby in Pasadena. Dale and Robin were screened thoroughly by Shirley's mother and selected to be her playmates. If there was anything suspicious to be found about the family or the boys, Gertrude Temple's investigation would have discovered it before she allowed the boys to be Shirley's playmates. Dale remained friends with Shirley and her husband on into the '60s.

Norman reminisced that Winona was a concert-level pianist. He always held great love for her. In his last years in Sweden, he was certain she had reincarnated there and doted on the child. Winona was never of robust health and had heart issues as she got older, with a bad heart attack in 1947. She was a gentle soul, and the kids all report feeling loved and safe with her. She worked hard at Murphy Ranch like most of the others, and the move to Ramona in 1945 at the end of the Murphy Ranch time was partly to make life easier for her. She was frequently bedridden at that time. Her heart issues finally caught up with her, and she died on September 3, 1954.

Norman and Winona, early 1950s.   *Stevens Family Archives*

4 MURPHY RANCH AND WORLD WAR II

The 1920s were good years for the Stevens family for the most part. But they were increasingly frightened by the onset of the Great Depression at the close of the decade and the worsening situation around the world in the 1930s. Winona was convinced by her spiritual advisor Conrad Anderson (Chapter 6) that they needed to take special action to protect the family from whatever was coming. In 1933, while Norman was away in Canada looking after some mining interests, Winona purchased the 40+ acre Murphy Ranch from Jessie Murphy to build a self-sufficient retreat for the family. Jessie Murphy became a friend of Winona's. Theanne remembers visiting her with Winona, in a Santa Monica apartment, when Jessie was in bed with illness.

The Stevens preferred their privacy as wealthy people often do. They did not announce the purchase or their plan to set up a survival retreat with a farm, orchard, generator, etc. Instead, they let it appear that Jessie Murphy still owned the ranch and that Norman was just serving as her main engineer in designing the facility. Even in correspondence with their famous neighbor, Will Rogers, Norman presents himself as the property engineer for Jessie Murphy.

Norman and Winona hired architects to draw up plans for a four-story mansion. Several plans were created by the firm of Plummer, Wurdeman, and Becket, starting in 1933. In 1939 they hired the famous architect Paul R. Williams, a Black man. Many times, I have read the comment online: "Isn't it ironic that these Nazis hired a Black architect?" The correct statement is: "Isn't it moronic to think that Nazis would hire a Black architect?"

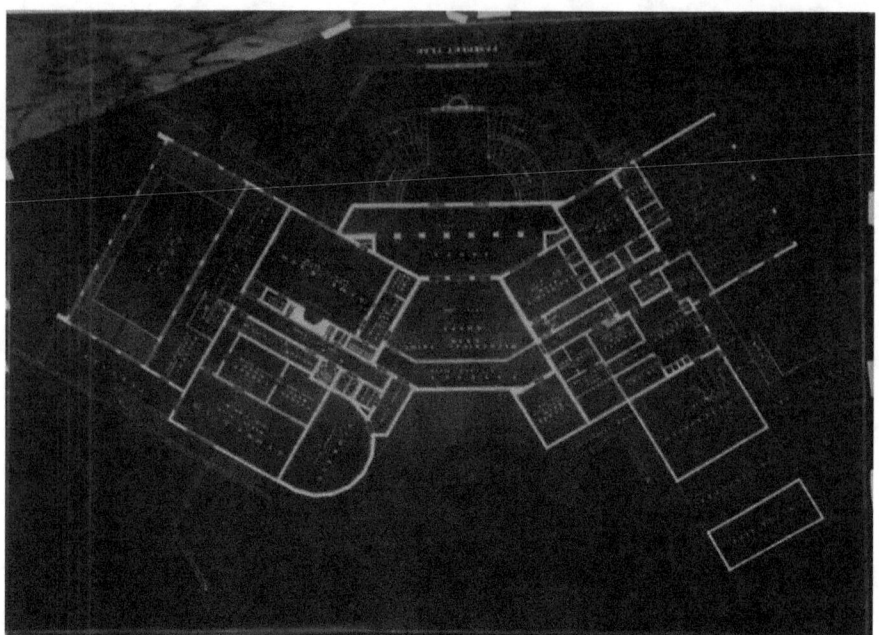

Basement plan   *Huntington Library*

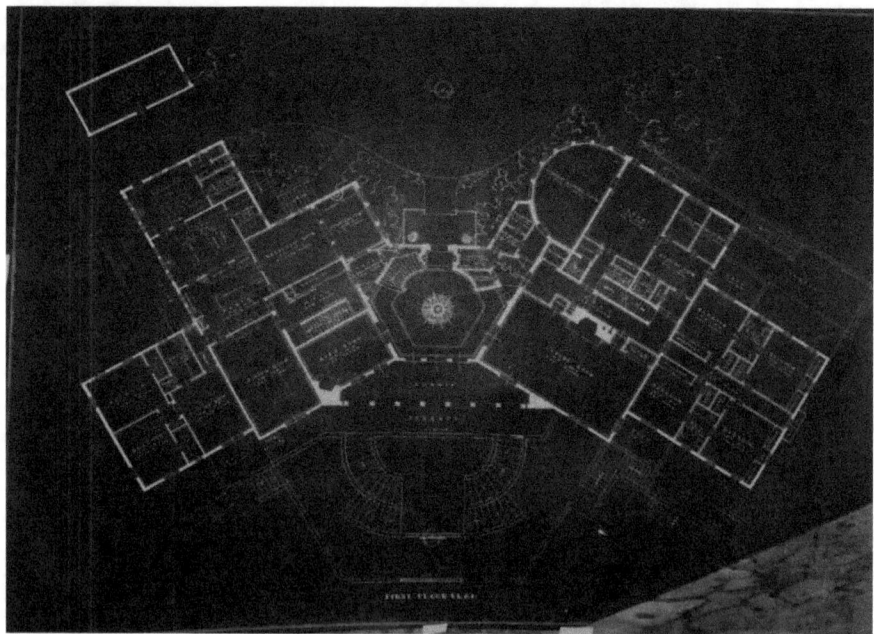

First-floor plan   *Huntington Library*

A later design   *Stevens Family Archives*

Construction of the facilities at Murphy Ranch, official address 2800 Rustic Canyon Road, took about eight years, 1933-1941. The project employed dozens of people at any given date, helping the Depression economy in the region. It was a tremendous amount of work to channel the creek, terrace the hillsides, build the nine long concrete staircases, clear the land, set up irrigation to all the terraces, and build the initial structures. The powerhouse is the only remaining building as of 2023.

The 1930s were memorable years in Los Angeles, beyond the spectacular movies produced there. As in Europe and the rest of America, the Great Depression affected nearly everyone. The enormous numbers of unemployed and underemployed were a dissatisfied voter base that political ideologues tried to harness. Communism, Socialism, and even National Socialism, the Nazi party, were all legal and active political parties alongside the Republican and Democratic parties. In Los Angeles, a branch of the national "Silver Legion of America", nicknamed the "Silver Shirts", formed. The national group was founded by Nazi supporter William Dudley Pelley. It harnessed antisemitism and fascist tendencies, and Pelley imbued the philosophy with a spiritual twist that the German Nazis were very skeptical of; he received little support from them.

The Communist Party was also quite active in Los Angeles in the 1930s, marching and leafletting, recruiting the working class. They were beaten severely and often by Los Angeles Police but remained vocal. Whether the workers at Murphy Ranch were recruited into this or other workers' movements is an open question.

Wartime Los Angeles was an exciting place for the boys in the Stevens family. Robin tells the story of watching American airplanes bomb a Japanese submarine off Redondo Beach on Christmas Day, 1941. An anchored barge not far offshore, used for fishing, was sunk in the process, and the sub got away. There were nightly "blackouts" if you can imagine trying to stop all light coming from Los Angeles. Aircraft factories, such as Lockheed and Douglas Aircraft, were camouflaged to look like alfalfa fields and farms from the air.

The Stevens family didn't move to Murphy Ranch until well after the war broke out. Conrad Anderson had already moved in, a year or two before.

Thanksgiving Day, 1942, without forewarning, the children were told to pack a few things, they were leaving their Hermosa Beach house to live at Murphy Ranch, and they would not be coming back. They left that evening. Theanne cried for days over leaving her friends and school. Carlile was excited about getting to operate all the machinery. Carlile and Theanne did continue going to a different school. They walked or were driven by Winona to and from a nearby elementary school, roughly 2 miles away. They played with Blackie and Brownie, the two dogs on the ranch. The kids were up at 5 AM each day. Carlile's job each morning was to set all the gopher traps. Then Winona would drive them to school, pick them up at 3 PM, they would work on more chores until dark. Then dinner, homework, and to bed. They were not allowed to do things with friends outside of school.

Life on the ranch was hard work for everyone except Conrad Anderson. Even with a hired hand or two, it was a lot of work to maintain the roads, power, plumbing, orchards, and many farm animals. The children, despite the wealth of their parents, worked as hard as children in a farm family. Theanne was 10, Carlile 11, Robin 15, and Dale 17 when they moved in. Carlile remembers with pride successfully handling the duty of running the giant diesel generators when he was just 11 years old. He sometimes had to sleep in the Power House to make sure the power never failed. The sound of a diesel engine starting to sputter would wake him, and he would start the second generator engine before the first failed. It took all his body weight to get the wheel spinning to start it.

Gulliver the bull was large, frightening, and afraid of nothing - except, fortunately, a squirt from the water hose. His pen was made of wire cables strung between fence posts nearly as wide as telephone poles. Robin tells of the bull setting his horns in the cables and slowly lifting the giant fence posts right out of the ground.

Winona did laundry and washing but was not the only wealthy adult hard at work. Josephine Spotts, an heiress and follower of Conrad Anderson, was seventy years old and fed the rabbits and churned butter. Ilsa Reynolds, of a similar background, did the cooking. Maybe these wealthy people were fulfilled by laboring with their hands.

My young father and his brothers ran up and down the long concrete staircases along the side of the canyon as they did their chores. Robin held a shovel out in front of him when he went up and down those stairs, and it paid off, once a rattlesnake struck at the shovel. The nine staircases are still there, in good shape despite over seventy years of weathering. All are several hundred steps, at least, the longest is over five hundred steps. It is hard to grasp how long this is without trying to walk it. To give you some comparison, the Empire State Building has 1576 steps up the 86 stories of stairs.

Three acres in the bottomlands were planted with alfalfa for the livestock.

There were cows (serviced by Gulliver to produce calves and milk), goats, chickens, and ducks. Gabriel the mule had the job of helping haul manure up to the terraces to fertilize the trees. Carlile says this mule would stop immediately when it heard the word "whoa" or any word with the "oh" sound in it.

Norman spoke proudly of the 20,000-gallon diesel fuel tank and the 10,000-gallon lubricating oil tank. There is also a buried gasoline tank. He succeeded in making the place self-sufficient. The only connection to the outside world was a phone line. In 1938 there was a fire nearby, and the fire department wanted to use the water in the big water tank. But no one answered the phone; they finally broadcast a plea on the radio and someone in the construction crew at Murphy Ranch heard it and opened the gates for them.

When it appeared that Dale might be drafted for World War II, Conrad set out to preserve his labor. He had Winona try to arrange an agricultural exemption, and it almost worked. One day, the story goes, the Army representatives came to Murphy Ranch to talk with her about it and see the farm. They were ready to agree to the exemption. After all, it was a huge farm to maintain. But before they left, Dale slipped away, ran up one of the staircases, and managed to catch the Army men at the gate as they were leaving the ranch. "Take me with you, I want to enlist!" He begged them, and that was the end of the agricultural exemption.

Dale Stevens fought in Patton's army, marching toward Germany. The story in the family is that he was a driver for Patton. He was awarded a purple heart for an injury he received under fire as an artillery spotter. An explosion lifted him ten feet in the air. He participated in the liberation of POW camps. He stayed on with the Army reserve, served during the Korean War, and was a 1st lieutenant when he died in 1996. That is according to his tombstone, the family thinks he held a higher rank. He was probably spared the frustration of hearing the Nazi story.

Robin served in the militarized Merchant Marine in the Pacific during World War II, supporting US troops in Japan right after the atomic bombs were dropped and Japan surrendered. His Liberty Ship, the John Paul Jones, was first in line to bring supplies to the Japanese mainland, bringing beer, Coca-Cola, cigarettes, and gasoline. He was particularly upset with the Nazi story, as Dale would have been.

I'm sure Norman never heard the story; he died in February 1993, after spending the last years of his life in Sweden. He had worked for Douglas Aircraft during the war, testing fighter planes that land on aircraft carriers, and had saved the lives of many pilots with his design improvements to the planes. The Secretary of the Navy was touring Douglas Aircraft at one point and asked to meet Norman. He congratulated Norman on a bracket he had developed that better connected the tails to the planes. His son Carlile (Steve) carried on this kind of work, developing improvements for the tail of the F-100 fighter plane in the 1950s.

Norman told the story of one way he determined what improvements the fighter planes needed. He had a newly built plane hauled up in the air thirty feet above the concrete floor of a hanger and ordered the men to drop it. There was a lot of resistance to this plan, the planes cost many thousands of 1940s dollars each to build. But he insisted, and I know how hard it would have been to argue with him when he was determined. They dropped the plane and learned just what damage the pilots would be facing when they tried to drop out of the sky quickly onto an aircraft carrier. This led to key design improvements.

The only thing Norman ever said to me about Nazis was "They were real stinkahs!" He was born in Maine and had the accent all his life. As I have said earlier, the idea of this patriotic and loving man ever being a "Nazi sympathizer" is ridiculous.

5 INVESTIGATING MURPHY RANCH

If you have ever been involved in a story which is later reported in the media, you know just how far off the reporting can be. Usually, many things are plain wrong, and are never corrected because no one wants to revisit "old news." It is strange to read story after story about Murphy Ranch that I know to be false, even though presented as solid journalism. And journalists double-check all their facts, right? Well, it was time for us to investigate for ourselves.

Over the years, I had heard many stories about "The Canyon", as they called it, from my father and grandfather. That was all I knew about it until the Nazi stories cropped up. And I heard about the mysterious Conrad Anderson and will tell of his role in Chapter 6. Not once were Nazis mentioned. No suspicions were confirmed, the kids had never heard an inkling about Nazis and their parents having anything to do with them.

My wife Valerie and I wanted to visit this place, so famous within our family and infamous in the press. As I wrote about earlier, I decided to bring the family together to learn about it. In May 2014, we all met for a week in a rented house in Woodland Hills, CA, not far from Murphy Ranch. Rustic Canyon, which Murphy Ranch is part of, was a quick drive for us down Topanga Canyon to the ocean, south along the coast for a half mile or so, and then a few miles of Sunset Boulevard winding up through Pacific Palisades. My father, Carlile (Steve) Stevens flew from Texas, and my uncle Robin Stevens from New York. My brother Todd Stevens flew with Valerie and I from Seattle to Los Angeles to join in the adventure.

As we researched and prepared for the trip, it became clear the person to talk to was Randy Young. Randy had been telling the story of Murphy Ranch and Rustic Canyon, even giving talks on it that included the Nazi legend, ever since his mother Betty Lou Young had written about it for her book Rustic Canyon and the Story of the Uplifters, in 1975. Besides some of the actual architectural diagrams, the information about the misspelled "Stephens" family was mainly speculative. No one had contacted the family, though Norman was still alive then and could have told the real story. And the Stevens family had not contacted the Youngs, so the Youngs can't be blamed for repeating for 40 years what others had told them.

I emailed the authors of articles about Murphy Ranch, and those who had interviewed Randy but had no luck finding him that way. There were too many "Randy Young" listings to try to find a phone number. I also called lots of people to try to see who could let us in the gate; my father and uncle in their 80s weren't going to walk a mile down the road and back in the blazing sun. Finally, I reached Stephen Bylin, the Sector Superintendent of the Topanga Parks system. He not only arranged for the gate to be opened for us but was also able to put me in touch with Randy Young.

I try to be ethical and honest. So, I had a dilemma in calling Randy. I did not know him yet and was concerned that if I told him of my relationship with the Ranch, he would be afraid the family was out to get him for his stories associating us with Nazis. He might even think that we were Nazis and refuse to meet with me. Not to mention, the story he would tell me would likely be very different from the one he had been telling everyone else, and I wanted to hear him tell the story just as he always had.

I decided being honest didn't mean I had to blurt out everything. When we finally spoke over the phone, just in time before our trip south to California from Washington State, I told him I was writing a book about wartime Los Angeles and wanted to interview him. This was true enough, if not the whole truth. I admit that if he had asked if I was related to the ranch's former owners, I would have said "I spell my name with a 'v'," and hoped that would be answer enough. After all, the story he told again and again spelled the family name "Stephens." But he didn't ask. Instead, he very generously offered to give us a tour of the ranch and tell us the whole story as we went! We took him up on the offer. It was a day I remember vividly.

Valerie, Todd, and I parked in the beautiful Pacific Palisades neighborhood nicknamed "The Riviera." It has some of the most expensive homes in the Los Angeles area. The streets are named after places on the Italian Coast: Capri, Amalfi, Monaco, Sorrento, and Napoli. Randy met us there and turned out to be an affable, energetic person despite his white hair, with incredible resistance to extreme heat, as we were about to discover. Again, determined to be straight with him, I told him we had information about Murphy Ranch he might not have. He stopped me right there, saying "Wait until after we walk, you can tell me then." What a relief! It was to go exactly as I had hoped, with Randy telling the story everyone else had heard over the years. Todd managed to videotape the entire walk with Randy, some of which is posted on https://murphyranch.org. And Randy signed a release form! Thank you, Randy.

The road skirted the high side of the canyon, soon leaving the houses behind, as well as the trees to shade us from the hot sun. Randy pointed back to the houses overlooking the canyon, identifying the homes of Steven Spielberg, Tom Hanks, Steven Bochco, and other famous and/or rich people. The last house we passed was that of Winston Salzer, a co-founder of Amgen. Shading our eyes from the sun, we could now see out to the hazy ocean. The smell of hot chaparral filled the air. After a mile or so, there was the chain link fence with three strands of barbed wire at the top, marking the high corner of Murphy Ranch, which sloped down to our left. Coming from the cool shorelines of Washington State, we were dripping sweat and sunscreen. Even the breeze was hot, and there was little shade. Not much further was a gap in the fence and a concrete staircase descending out of sight into undergrowth far below. We followed heat-proof Randy down the endless steps into Murphy Ranch, a place he has visited perhaps hundreds of times since he first explored it in the 1970s.

Ocean view from the road to Murphy Ranch   *Photo: Valerie Stevens*

As we walked, Randy told us many stories we had read online, and some we hadn't heard. We tried not to shake our heads in disbelief when he said Winona was the daughter of Jessie Murphy. We learned about the Silver Shirts, a Nazi group active in Los Angeles in the 30s. He mentioned mysterious goings-on, such as séances. Somehow these stories blended with the Nazi stories about the ranch. He told the story of Herr Schmidt, and a "wanted" poster for him, reprinted later in this book. Schmidt had supposedly been the German agent who convinced my grandparents to build the ranch for Nazi purposes. Randy agreed that he could find no evidence for the story of Herr Schmidt's arrest in an FBI raid the day after Pearl Harbor.

Randy mentioned bizarre things that had happened at Murphy Ranch in its more recent history: porno films, rock and roll videos, devil worshipers gathering. He identified some of the fragrant sages and sumacs we smelled and told us the history of neighboring properties and the Pacific Palisades region.

The first look at the ranch was like walking into a bizarre, multicolored version of the family stories.

Incinerator   *Photo: Valerie Stevens*

The main house arches and ruins.   *Photo: Valerie Stevens*

At last, we returned to our cars. I suggested to Randy that we go to a restaurant to talk further; he proposed a nearby park. Once there, video camera recording, I told him who I was, and asked him if he wanted to meet two people who had lived there in the 1940s. I told him much more about my grandparents than he had known and gave him the information he had been trying to find for 40 years. He said the hairs on the back of his neck were standing up. After all, to hear nothing from the inhabitants for all this time while he told the history he thought he knew, and then suddenly have the family appear with a different story made for a big moment. I told him he could meet two people who had grown up there, my father and uncle. As a historian, genuinely interested in knowing what happened, he eagerly accepted and met with all of us a couple of days later. He told us he had heard that some descendants were in the Seattle area, likely it was us he had heard about, so he was a bit prepared.

When Randy visited, we were all in for some surprises. Randy gave us a copy of the affidavit signed by John Vincent (who had helped Huntington Hartford buy the property from the Stevens in 1949) that was the origin of Randy's version of the Nazi tale. He said that when he and his mother spoke to John Vincent's wife Ruth in 1975, Ruth said she wanted to protect her friend Winona and refused to give them her phone number. Carlile pointed out that Winona had died in his arms in 1954. Ruth for some reason believed or pretended she was still alive.

Randy had copies of some correspondence between Will Rogers and his wife, and the Stevens. There had been a dispute over the culvert Norman had built to guide water through the Murphy Ranch property. The Rogers and their grounds superintendent were afraid it would cause flooding or decrease groundwater for the Rogers place just downstream from Murphy Ranch. Norman answered the correspondence as Jesse Murphy's superintendent, even though by this time he and Winona owned the property. The matter was closed when Will Rogers died on August 15, 1935, in a plane crash in Alaska. The letters are posted on https://murphyranch.org.

In my research, I was surprised to find a first-hand account of someone who met Norman at Murphy Ranch. He is a fascinating person – Charles Bennett, a British actor and screenwriter who wrote for Hitchcock and others. He somehow became part of a mounted patrol in the California State Militia and patrolled the Santa Monica mountains on horseback during World War II. Here is his account of meeting Norman Stevens at Murphy Ranch, from the book "Hitchcock's Partner in Suspense", by Bennett's son John Charles Bennett.

"I have learned recently of a National Park Service plaque which states that a wartime spy lived up Rustic Canyon in the Santa Monica Mountains. Swastikas were found painted on the interior walls of a generator shed, and there was evidence of radio equipment. I knew that property well. It was located upstream of the Will Rogers ranch, and it belonged to a senior Douglas test engineer, Norman Stevens, who was troubleshooting bombers before the Battle of Midway. He had installed the generators to power his house and irrigate his orchard — there was no other source of electricity — where he intended to lie low with his family if the Japanese invaded. Our troop frequently scouted down through the dense thickets of sumac adjacent to his property — and I recall meeting the engineer. But our patrols were on public land, so I cannot speak to the unlikely truth of what the Park Service found on his private property.

I suppose it possible that a foreign agent could spy on this important engineer while working as his farmhand. I also suppose that painted swastikas might be construed as evidence of spying - though a spy who would so advertise is a fool. Certainly, the possession of radio equipment is no crime, particularly if assembled by a brilliant, reclusive engineer. But I have a more likely explanation. The engineer was a prominent theosophist, a cult that finds special significance in that very ancient swastika symbol. So maybe his handyman, perhaps an occultist, painted swastikas with his employer's approval. Of course, this does not rule out spying, or any mystical art. But one thing is for certain: the conjecture of a psychic saboteur targeting Douglas Aircraft provides an intriguing story I should have written but did not."

I highly recommend this book, published in 2014, to anyone interested in

Hollywood of the 30s, 40s, and 50s, as well as wartime England. Most is written by Charles Bennett himself, an energetic and witty observer of the times, who also played an active role in the middle of Hollywood's golden years. His skepticism about the Nazi tale is refreshing.

I have not found mention of the plaque he refers to anywhere else. It is an odd piece of the puzzle. This plaque, if it existed, would be evidence of an earlier version of the story, and the plaque itself may have fueled the rumors John Vincent picked up on.

In 1949, Norman and Winona sold the property to Huntington Hartford, 37 years old at the time, an heir to the large A&P supermarket fortune. John Vincent, a UCLA music professor, assisted. Robin Stevens remembered him as an odd, shy person who would sit away from everyone else in the room, not facing them, while his agents discussed business with Norman and Winona. Hartford was paid $1.5 million a year by his uncles. My family's story is that he was paid to stay out of the A&P business. He had many millions of dollars and spent his money on art museums and extravagant projects such as the one to make Murphy Ranch into an artist's colony. He bought the adjoining Josepho property, too, for a total of 150 acres. He hired architect Lloyd Wright, who designed two more buildings, and some cottages, and re-used existing buildings. The colony opened in 1951. Artists, composers, writers, and craftspeople were given scholarships for one to six-month retreats. Christopher Isherwood, Andrew Wyeth, Henry Miller, and others were among those who stayed there. Note that none of the writers said anything about a Nazi past, I'm sure they never heard anything about it, or they would have. Jewish artist Bizinsky stayed there, others to whom the past would have mattered. But there is no discussion of Nazis at the ranch at all in the 1950s press.

Hartford dated Lana Turner. When he broke up with her, she complained that she had already had towels monogrammed "H. H." He replied that she should date Howard Hughes. Which she did!

Hartford lost money on nearly everything he did. When asked about it, he said: "I had money. I didn't need to make money." He died in 2008, fortune gone, an interesting example of what someone might do when handed a huge fortune. He was a philanthropist and a drug addict and was also relieved of great sums by unscrupulous people.

John Vincent helped with the sale and ran the artist colony. He appears to be the main source of the Nazi rumors, which we will explore in a later chapter.

There were Nazis in LA in the 1930's, and across the country. Rachel Maddow recently did a podcast series about them, https://www.msnbc.com/rachel-maddow-presents-ultra. They were a much greater threat and impact than people realize these days. There were elected officials that supported them, too. There are two books about Nazis in Los

Angeles: *Hitler in Los Angeles*, by Steven J. Ross, and *Hollywood's Spies*, by Laura B. Rosenzweig. Certainly, the Nazis existed in the 1930s, but I am just as certain that Norman and Winona Stevens were not among them.

Huntington Hartford   photo Diane Hartford   *Creative Commons Attribution-Share Alike 3.0 Unported*

6 CONRAD ANDERSON

In 1931, four-year-old Robin Stevens was very sick. The skin infection "impetigo" covered his body with numerous sores, and his life was threatened by it. He had to be isolated because it was so contagious. Norman and Winona were distraught and tried every treatment of the time. Winona spent a year following the treatment proscribed by Christian Science, which was Theophila's religion, and to that point Norman and Winona's. The treatment involved a lot of praying, but no doctors. After a year of no improvement, Winona was desperate, and Norman was fed up with Christian Science. He forcefully took Robin from the people who kept and prayed for him. Norman had heard of someone through friends, a Norwegian healer of unusual ability, Conrad Anderson.

They brought Anderson to see Robin in the big house in Pasadena. He bent over Robin's bed and touched his sores; Robin remembered the tingling sensation and told us about it as an old man. Then Anderson announced that all the sores would be healed in a week. And they were, all except for a few sores in Robin's hairline Anderson could not see. From this point forward Conrad Anderson could do no wrong in Winona's eyes. She gave up Christian Science and adopted Anderson as the spiritual guide for the Stevens family. He had a strong accent from his Norwegian origins in the Lofoten islands. All agree he had a powerful presence and a combination of charisma and certainty in his abilities, which was very convincing. Norman said Anderson had incredible abilities to concentrate and meditate. He was also older, 54 in 1933, and took advantage of his seniority. Norman spent $10,000 setting up an office for Anderson on Occidental Blvd in Los Angeles, called "The Arcane School of Health."

The ARCANE
School of Health
235 So. Occidental Blvd.
Los Angeles

Letterhead   *Stevens Family Archives*

The family was probably unaware Conrad had been taken to court for practicing medicine without a license in 1930, though it was reported in several newspapers. He had claimed to be treating a woman with cosmic rays emanating from his fingertips and charged the couple $1200. The woman had been very ill and died. It was 90 days in jail or a $500 fine; he paid the fine. Norman and Winona proved too trusting, and not for the last time.

Anderson advised the family on many things and told them there would be another war, one he could help prepare them for. Winona suspected he was right and was worried for their children. Anderson assured them he had the power to protect them if they did as he said. He suggested to Winona that they build a self-sufficient retreat in the hills north of Los Angeles, so she bought the Murphy Ranch property. Eventually, the construction of a functioning farm and retreat appealed to the engineer in Norman. He returned from his prospecting and mining efforts in Canada and set to work planning it; construction was underway by the end of 1934. The first house on the ranch was built for Conrad Anderson, and he moved in before the rest of the family, around 1939-40.

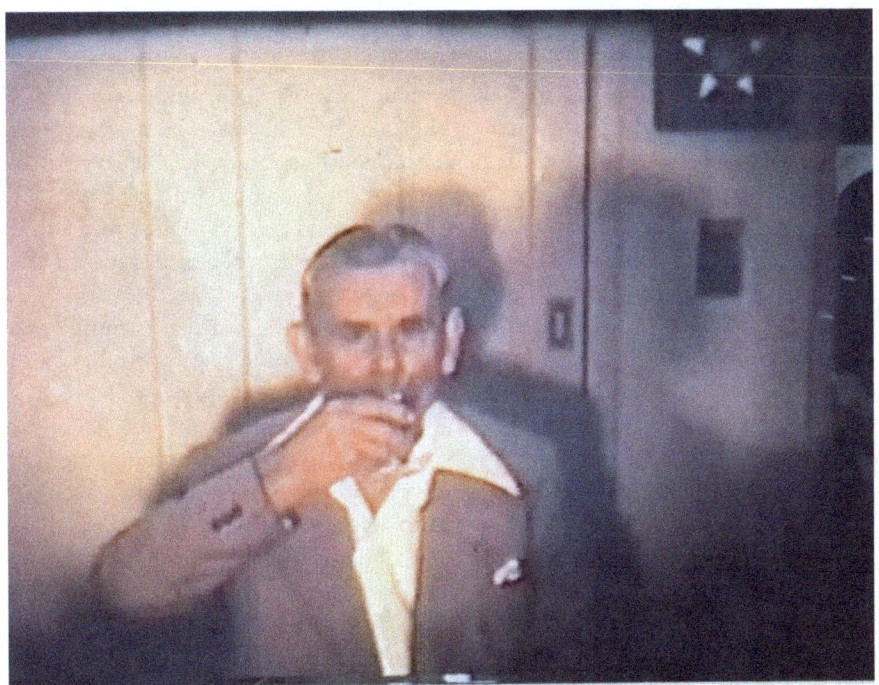

Conrad Anderson, from a 16mm movie filmed at Murphy Ranch in 1941   Stevens Archives

Conrad Anderson with Blackie and Brownie, just puppies.   Stevens Family Archives

Does the story of how Conrad Anderson became involved with the Stevens family sound familiar? Twenty-five years earlier a similar story had played out in Imperial Russia. Czar Nicholas and his wife had a very sick child, Prince Alexis. A mysterious healer named Rasputin was able to control the child's hemophilia and was welcomed into the inner circles of the wealthy royal family. He took full advantage of his access, and his sexual and other adventures played a part in the discrediting and eventual destruction of the royal family, whether or not that had been his intention. Rasputin was mysterious to the end, proving difficult to kill. He was seemingly immune to poison and bullets shot at point-blank range. Eventually, more bullets and being thrown into the river finally did him in. The story is well known. Conrad Anderson's death was also unusual, as we shall see.

Anderson had followers; wealthy women who gave him presents, money, and assets. Two of these women moved to the ranch to be near him, Josephine Spotts and Ilsa Reynolds. They lived in the main house with the family, and Conrad in his own house. Ilsa ended up doing all the cooking. Jo Spotts milked cows and tended animals. This was quite a change from the wealthy society they were used to. Conrad's favorite, Florence Camp, did minimal work. She was a former beauty queen from Sweden and Anderson's closest associate. He eventually put her in charge of running the ranch's day-to-day operations. The children tell stories of her calling out orders from behind a dark window while she ate candy and steadily became more obese. She was listed as Anderson's contact on his 1940 draft registration.

Conrad Anderson, from a 16mm movie
filmed at Murphy Ranch in 1941   Stevens Family Archives

Anderson was not from a farming background. He discovered one day that the cows had no upper front teeth (no cow does). He was upset about it and thought the cows were defective. Another time, he was concerned the chickens were getting wet in the rain. Ed, a ranch hand, told him, "If God hadn't wanted chickens to get wet, he would have got little mackintoshes and booties for them." Conrad's talents were in the invisible realms; if anyone had a headache, they went to Anderson. He would put his hand on their head and the headache would go away.

The children were frightened of him, which he encouraged. In the 1930s, he put Dale and Robin through grueling "health" treatments like fasting for a week on juices, with daily colonics, and extreme heat treatments. Anderson threatened Carlile, saying if he didn't behave and do his many chores at the canyon, he would have his "Leena", a spaceship, pick Carlile up and take him to his laboratory, and he would never see his parents again. Carlile remembered once working very long into the night, scared Conrad would make good on one of his threats, finally to be told Conrad had relented. Once Carlile let the main water tank overflow, it was his job to keep it full. His punishment was to get only oatmeal to eat on his birthday. Of course, he ran up into the orchards and ate all the fruit he wanted.

Before the move to the ranch, he convinced Norman and Winona to send the two oldest boys away to Southwestern Academy, a full-time boarding school, for summers, too. Robin and Dale were only home for 2 weeks a year for several years in a row. Carlile wanted to be with his older brothers, and though Winona resisted, they sent him off full-time as well, at 6 years old. He was back home with the family full-time at Murphy Ranch.

We now know Anderson was also a sexual predator. He manipulated everyone he could and was a practitioner of black magic. He read books on black magic, explaining that when he did it, it became white magic because it was him doing it.

Anderson, with his accent and energy, was apparently a charming host at parties, could be very entertaining, and managed to keep Winona's trust until he died. He wanted the ranch and all the Stevens' assets; he had papers drawn up giving it all to him. The papers were found after his death, they only required Winona's signature. If his health had not betrayed him, he may have succeeded in completing his takeover. Conrad steadily worked at driving Norman off, saying his "energy" was bad for the ranch and the people. Unfortunately, he succeeded for years at a time; Norman went off to prospect for gold. When Norman returned, Conrad had Florence Kamp persuade Ilsa Reynolds to add arsenic to Norman's food daily, making him quite sick. Ilsa eventually confessed. When Norman didn't die, they panicked and flushed the remaining poison down the toilet.

Some people could have mistaken his Norwegian accent for a German accent, possibly giving rise to the story of a "Herr Schmidt" convincing

Winona to buy Murphy Ranch. A "bad" person indeed convinced her to buy it, though it doesn't seem likely Conrad was a Nazi. It is hard to know what he may have told people about himself, however.

Carlile reported that the family's concern during the war was about the Japanese, not the Germans. When they asked Conrad about the Japanese, he said not to worry: "If they come too close, I will use my powers to turn all their rice into rat droppings!"

Anderson died on the ranch on Dec 21, 1943. Carlile said Conrad was "burning" over the last months of his life. He spent his days in a bathtub full of ice water, feeling as if his skin was on fire. Theanne (Toni) says she was at school shortly after Conrad died, she heard another boy talking about something strange his father, a doctor, had seen. The doctor had been called to the bedside of a dead man who seemed to have severe burns covering most of his body, even though nothing else in the room, sheets or drapes, showed signs of fire. As the boy told the story, Theanne realized it was about Conrad Anderson. His death certificate does not mention burns, just a coronary event, so this is not corroborated. But several members of the family reported about Anderson saying he was burning up toward the end of his life, and the ice baths. Maybe messing with black magic was a bad idea.

He left Florence Kamp in charge of the ranch operations. She and Winona had a falling out sometime later. My father told the story of working on something high on one of the staircases when he heard loud voices in the valley below – his mother Winona arguing with Mrs. Kamp. He had never heard his mother raise her voice before. He says he ran down the steps so fast he practically flew. He heard his mother tell Mrs. Kamp that, contrary to her opinion, the ranch belonged to her, and Mrs. Kamp could pack her stuff and leave.

After Conrad died, they found a trunk full of jewelry he had collected from his followers. Winona and Norman attempted to restore the items to their owners. Winona bought a house in Ramona for Jo Spotts and Ilsa Reynolds when the family moved there from the ranch in 1945. But that was not the last anyone heard or saw of Conrad Anderson. Years after he died, the family had moved out of the ranch and Norman was trying to sell it, without luck. J.D. Woodruff had been hired as a caretaker and lived on the ranch. J.D. told Norman that one moonless night he had been walking between buildings on the property and got lost. Then a fellow with a flashlight had come and showed him the way back to the buildings. Norman asked what the man had looked like, and J.D. described Conrad perfectly. Norman pressed on with the questions, and J.D. sheepishly admitted he could see dead people. Norman was no stranger to the idea of subtle bodies, or the idea of "ghosts". He asked J.D. if he knew anyone else in that state. J.D. said, "Sure, I know others." He agreed to Norman's suggestion that he ask one of them to escort Conrad off the property. Norman had struggled to sell the property for years, but the next day, the story goes, the agreement to sell it to Huntington Hartford came together. It was completed in 1949. And Conrad Anderson was heard from no more.

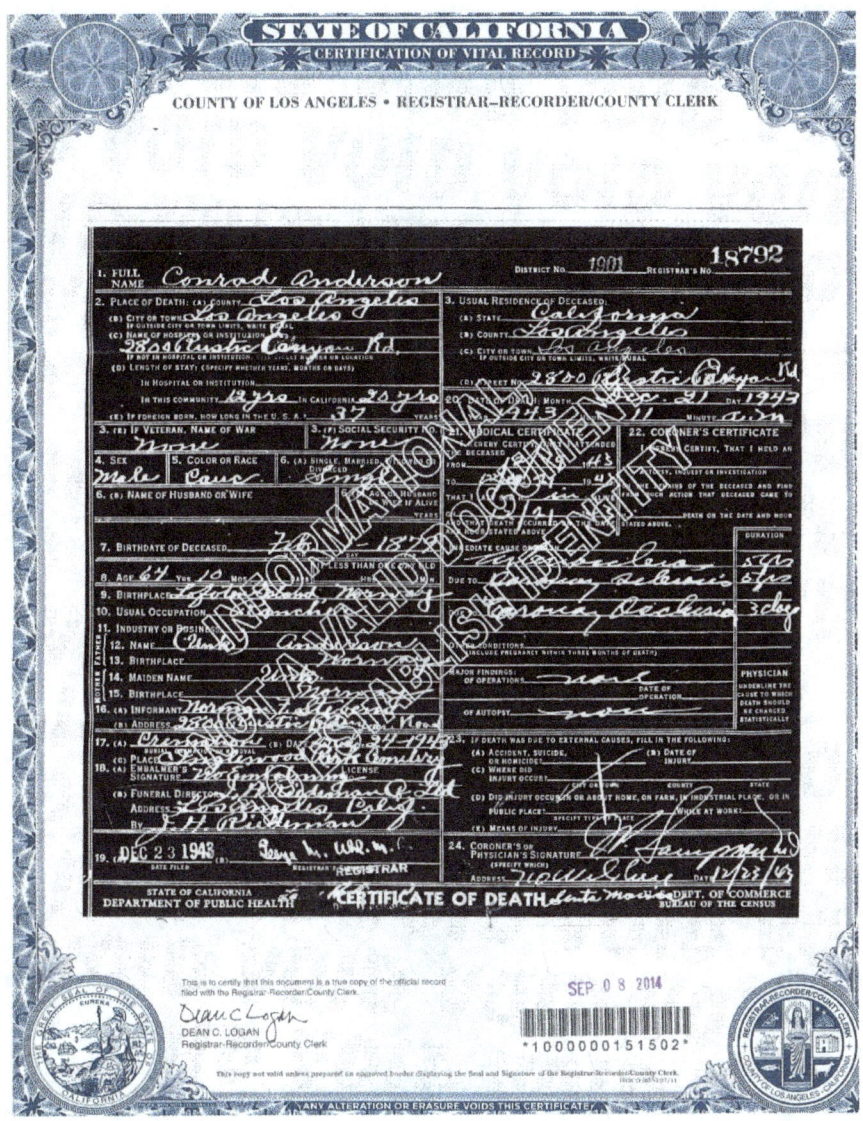

7 LOSING A LARGE FORTUNE

As a grade schooler in Los Angeles, I read about Sutter's Mill and the great California gold rush of 1849. They say it was like the entire continent was tilted with the East Coast raised – everyone who was loose rolled to the West Coast. Gold was a very hot topic in the 1930s, too. It was illegal to own any quantity of it more than personal jewelry. But people planning to survive a world crisis prefer to have gold and silver stashed away. Then, just as today, there was no certainty that paper money would retain its value in a big enough crisis, financial or other. So, Norman somehow bought a fortune in twenty-dollar and smaller gold pieces. He filled twenty half-gallon mason jars with them, and had Robin bury them at Murphy Ranch, on the slope toward the creek from the house they were living in, below the honeysuckle bush. Sometime later, Norman asked Robin to dig them up and bury them somewhere else on the grounds, to be better hidden. Robin did so, and for a time he was the only one who knew the location.

Often the friends of rich people don't turn out to be friends at all. Such was the case – a couple who knew about the gold threatened to turn Norman and Winona in to the government. I suppose it was straight-up blackmail, they wanted money or the gold. Norman asked Robin where the gold was buried, and Robin never saw it again. The story goes that Norman dug it up and his acquaintance Farmer Page helped him get rid of it, though probably for only 10 cents on the dollar of the day's value since it was illegal to own at the time.

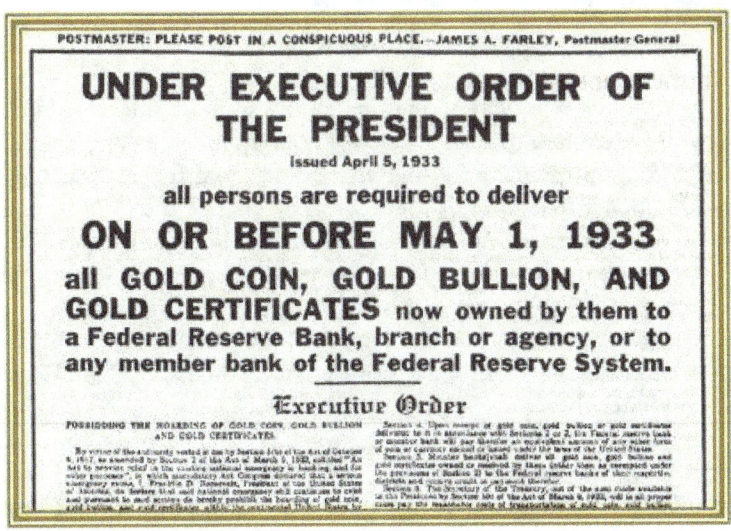

59

If you know something of Los Angeles history, the name "Farmer Page" will ring a bell. He ran ships for offshore gambling and drinking, out past the 3-mile limit during Prohibition. When that was finally shut down, he was one of the very first to invest in casinos in Las Vegas. He had a Midas touch, according to the family stories. When he had too much money to launder, he invested in large date farms, sure they would lose enough money to shelter his excess income. But they did quite well, and he had more money than ever to deal with. Page was always a gentleman, and never got in serious trouble since he was liked by the authorities.

Milton "Farmer" Page   photo: Los Angeles Daily News Negatives, Library Special Collections, Charles E. Young Research Library, UCLA

Are you wondering what twenty half-gallon mason jars full of gold coins is worth? If you are excited to read about gold buried in what is now a public place, let me warn you against a full-blown case of "gold fever". I would not be telling you about it if I thought there was any chance the gold remained on Murphy Ranch. Norman was no fool and needed money later in his life. He would not let a fortune remain buried where others could find it. After all, he prospected for gold for part of his life, and, according to him, in a prior life, too! And I talked it over thoroughly with Robin Stevens, who buried it twice. I know where to look, and have done so, just to be sure. I am no fool, either. It is no longer there.

It is fun to think there might be a huge fortune lurking in the immediate future, just like holding a lottery ticket in your hand. Before our first visit to the ranch in May 2014, we let ourselves get a bit excited about the extremely small possibility maybe one jar, maybe all of them, was still buried. How many one-ounce gold pieces might fit in a half-gallon Mason jar? Not the usual quart jar, the bigger version. Maybe 400? Worth about $1800 each, a jar would be worth over three-quarters of a million dollars. Times twenty – it almost hurt to think about it. Why couldn't they have put one of those jars aside for their grandkids?

I talked about it a lot; so my wife Valerie got me a metal detector for Christmas. As the plans for our trip to Los Angeles and Murphy Ranch took shape, we knew a search for buried gold would be part of the adventure. Once we were there, Uncle Robin filled us in on the details and drew us a literal "treasure map". He was certain the gold had been dug up since the family had years to move out, but he agreed it was a reasonable precaution to look for it before telling anyone it had been there.

The day finally came as part of our 2014 visit to the ranch. I hopped right out of bed when the 4:00 AM alarm went off. Valerie, Todd, and I walked up the road to the ranch in the pre-dawn light, determined that if there was any gold to be found at Murphy Ranch, we would find it. It was cool, quiet, and fragrant with the nocturnal flowers blooming in the summer night. The graffiti artists were not up that early. We figured we would have several hours to ourselves.

Where people have lived, stuff is in the ground. Just below the surface near the houses were bits of strange electrical parts, springs, wires, pipes, screws, nails, and unidentifiable junk. We forgot the headphones that would have silenced the beep of the metal detector, and it beeped a lot. Only once did people walk by during our search, we hid the metal detector quickly when we heard them approaching. We expected graffiti artists to mind their own business, but it was two hikers. To our discomfort, one of them called out "Find any treasure?". Besides the metal detector, we used dowsing rods, which Valerie had proven her skill with, in some tests we did at home hiding a gold piece in the grass.

I'm afraid the highlight of the whole adventure was the discovery of a buried enamel bucket full of dirt. But I remember the moment vividly; something big was down there, and the three of us couldn't help our excitement as it was steadily revealed to be a container of some sort. Anyway, I did find a dime on the trail, and it is now carefully preserved as "the treasure of Murphy Ranch".

It got hot, little flies came out, we heard voices in the distance, and we realized we had searched enough. Sitting on a ledge overlooking the Power House, we contemplated our mission as we watched the taggers who had shown up. They took a break on top of the building to smoke a joint, then went back inside to finish painting over the image of an angel we had admired earlier. I took a moment to meditate on the question of whether anything was buried at Murphy Ranch for us to find and got the answer that everything of my family's that could be withdrawn, had been. The only valuable thing buried there was the miles of copper pipe for the sprinkler systems in the terraces up the sides of the canyon.

We had been careful not to mention our treasure hunt to anyone, even relatives, unless they were directly involved. We did not and still don't want to trigger a "gold rush" that fills the park with holes. And what if we *had* returned to the rental house to triumphantly set a dirty half-gallon jar full of gold on the table (and then another, and another...) in front of Steve and Robin? Would we have become like Humphrey Bogart's character from *Treasure of the Sierra Madre*? Could we have become paranoid and suspicious, and put "getting our fair share" ahead of family unity? Maybe we dodged a bullet. And we would probably have broken the law just taking it from Murphy Ranch, anyway. But I would like to have faced the challenge.

Certainly, it was a lot of gold to us. But, just like the $900,000 Norman and Winona spent on Murphy Ranch, it was only a small part of their fortune. I don't know where all the many millions went, though it was nearly all spent by the time Winona died in 1954. Here are some key events in the dispersion.

1929 – Norman had taken on the task of investing their money since Winona was busy with the children and looking after her mother. Winona had a degree in economics from Stanford, and Norman had no training with money. Norman decided the stock market was a fine place for a lot of it in the 1920s, at least 3 million. After all, the market kept going up. I'm sure he was proud of his returns for the last few years in the roaring 20s, profiting like a successful investor. He'd escaped World War I without a traumatic trip to the battlefields of Europe and married a super-wealthy woman. Things were going well. They were raising their two kids, Dale and Robin, born in 1925 and 1927, maybe this was the best time of their marriage.

But Norman did not completely trust the stock market. He watched it carefully, and in 1929, a week before the big crash in October, he decided it was time to get out. He called his broker and ordered that everything - millions of dollars in stock - be sold. The broker was shocked and took some convincing, but Norman stuck to his guns and said, "Sell it all!" So, the broker sold it. Such a big sale could have contributed to some degree to the crash itself. When Black Thursday came, and the chaotic days after, Norman was relieved to have sold. But the feeling was short-lived. The bank holding the proceeds of his sales had closed for good, like many others during the crash, and all of Norman's millions from stock sales disappeared.

The elaborate plans for a large mansion at Murphy Ranch were drawn up after this, in the 1930s, there was plenty of money left. And Murphy Ranch is where another chunk of it went. Beyond the $900,000 to build it, people were living there to support; the family, Conrad Anderson and his expenses, ranch hands, boarding school tuition for two of the three boys, and life for several years. In 1949, the ranch was sold at a huge loss to Huntington

Hartford, for $100,000.

Winona owned an entire square block of downtown Pasadena, right on Colorado Blvd. The kids remember watching the Rose Parade from the top of one of the buildings. Winona rode a horse in the parade in 1910 as a young woman. All six of the children were born in Pasadena, in the big house on La Loma Road, as mentioned earlier. But there is one unpleasant memory from Pasadena: when Winona's Pasadena real estate was stolen.

In the 1930s, Winona decided to sell one of their properties in Pasadena and was working out the sale with a real estate agent. The following story is told within the family. One day, the agent brought a lot of papers to Winona to sign regarding the sale. Maybe she was not well that day, or maybe she just thought it would be rude to question the real estate agent. But he had carefully prepared deeds of sale for all the property she owned in Pasadena, transferring ownership to him, and Winona signed the whole stack of papers without realizing what was in them. Maybe the courses at Stanford that were part of getting her degree in Economics did not teach how to avoid fraud. It seems both Norman and Winona trusted people far too easily, far too often.

When they discovered what this criminal real estate agent had done, they hired a lawyer to rectify things. Conrad Anderson recommended the lawyer. The crooked agent felt confident since he had Winona's signature on the deeds, so he fought back, and eventually, the case went to a jury trial. As the trial progressed, it became clear the lawyer Anderson had recommended was incompetent. Norman had done a lot of research and could see they were in trouble. In the courtroom, Norman was continually whispering to the lawyer with suggestions of what to do, and how to proceed. The crooked agent's lawyer seized on this, pointing out to the jury: "If these people are as naive as they claim, as they would have to be to make this supposed mistake, why is it they are advising their lawyer, rather than him advising them?" The jury bought it, and they lost the case. They even lost the appeal in 1945, which you can find online if you google "Stevens vs. Hutton." Reading the case, it seems quite different from the family story, it could be the wrong case, or it could be that Mr. Hutton's defense attorney managed to convince the court of an alternate story.

It appears they may have donated to causes they supported, such as the Lucis Trust, but we have no clear record. The last large expenditures were for property in and around Ramona, California, where the family moved in 1945 from Murphy Ranch. They bought the Montecito Ranch, acreage they called the "cactus farm," a nice house with acreage, and another ranch, 120 acres in total. All were eventually sold at a loss. They made big donations to the Lemurian Fellowship, based in Ramona. Howard Zitko was one of the founders. Ilsa Reynolds moved to the Fellowship's compound when Jo Spotts died. The story is, the Lemurians would not let anyone talk to her; she was old and had a $100,000 life insurance policy that would go to the

Fellowship.

My Uncle Robin told us that the kids had a hard time taking the Lemurian Fellowship seriously. He told us a story about a big ceremony that happened for Norman. He was to be told his Lemurian name, supposedly what he had been called millions of years ago in Lemuria. It was a big deal! With great solemnity, the ceremony reached its conclusion. It was announced, "Norman Stevens, your Lemurian name was... NOR STEFAN!" Oh, we laughed so hard.

There was some contribution to Stanford tuition for Carlile and Theanne, but Carlile had to earn the money to complete his degree. He did this with a great deal of ingenuity, giving science shows at state fairs, which included huge sparks from a 2-million-volt tesla coil he constructed himself.

It could be that their attitude was like that of Huntington Hartford, the playboy millionaire who purchased Murphy Ranch from the Stevens family. When Hartford was asked why he so consistently lost money on his investments, he said something to the effect: "I have money already, it is not a priority to me to get more. I intend to see what interesting things I can do with money, whether it makes more or not."

Norman was never comfortable with his wife's riches. He was determined to make his contribution to the family fortune. He prospected for gold in Canada, found a good claim on the Fraser River, and put some people he trusted in charge of it so he could spend time with his family in California. Again he trusted the wrong people, all was stolen. He prospected for uranium in Utah and met Ezra Taft Benson there, who would later be the head (the prophet) of the Mormon Church. He did not find uranium, however. He also started a foundry in Hermosa Beach, probably again to have his own business that contributed to the family's fortune. It could be he was relieved when Winona's fortune ran out, about the time she died in 1954. All that money had deprived him of the chance to support the family, given Winona's mother power over their lives, and attracted Conrad Anderson and other thieves. Norman was smart and hard-working; he would have had no problem supporting their family as an engineer.

A gecko Norman cast in his foundry.   *Photo: Stanton Stevens*

8 CONFRONTING AN URBAN LEGEND

Maybe Nazi myths just don't die. Maybe Nazis don't either; I've killed thousands of Nazi Zombies in video games, and there are always more coming.

When you want to know something these days, chances are you search the internet for it and find yourself looking at a Wikipedia page. There is even a Wikipedia page for Murphy Ranch. I have no idea why someone felt compelled to create it. It is fascinating; a textbook example of something untrue giving every appearance of being true. There are many references, with authoritative-sounding text repeating the usual stories, even the later whoppers tacked on by who knows who. All the references trace back to the single story told by Randy Young and his mother's book. But if the LA Times, Slate, the Huffington Post, and many different articles repeat the same thing, then it must be true, right?

Some don't trust Wikipedia because, supposedly, anyone can add and modify the text there. But I found the opposite to be the case. Someone who knows what really happened can't post it on Wikipedia; I tried and failed. Leaving the urban myth text intact, I posted an addition:

"Note from a reader: most of this tale is urban legend. Besides the ruins of buildings that don't tell much about the people who lived there, there is no factual evidence for any of the Nazi stories or articles, not even a newspaper article about the supposed detainment of 50 caretakers. The many references in the information above circle back on themselves, and originate in one person, Randy Young. They prove the point that "most history is the history of gossip." It is interesting to observe how readily people (and newspapers!) declare hearsay to be fact. No one who lived there during the 30s and World War II has come forward to say anything at all. I know several people who lived there during that time and will set the entire story straight soon with a book, hopefully. I'm afraid that people would rather believe glamorous stories about Nazis than about ordinary, if wealthy, people. The real story is more interesting, though than the Nazi fiction. I hope that those who read this while doing research for an article will be better able to avoid the mistakes that reporters have made so far regarding this story."

But my comments were unwelcome; the power of others to remove text trumped my ability to add it. Only 13 hours later, someone deleted my text with the non-sequitur "This article was literally just one person ranting about the government and Nazis. I've deleted it." As if "one person" can know nothing! And I hadn't mentioned the government at all! So, I boldly put my text back to see what would happen next, with the following comment

"Restoring what was added, since it is legitimately about the content, and more accurate than the existing content."

This attempt survived only about 21 hours. Another anonymous censor removed my words again, with the comment: "Removed section that violates multiple parts of Wikipedia rules. You can't use Wikipedia to post original research." I had to give up at this point. Wikipedia has a rule: only references to other published material can be used. Of course, every kind of nonsense imaginable has been published, most of it referring to other published nonsense. Once this book is published, I will finally have a reference to give in Wikipedia and will try again to correct the page.

It is a Frankenstein's monster of a story, impossible to control. Even Randy Young declares that much of what is currently stated in published articles is embellishments and exaggerations. He says that even before he heard the real story from us, he had to assert repeatedly that there was no intention for Murphy Ranch to be "Hitler's headquarters in the US," and that Jessie Murphy did indeed exist and wasn't just a fictional character cooked up by the Stevens'.

Here is a nutshell summary of the urban legend, with the most common embellishments. **Nothing of the following summary is true!**

> *Murphy Ranch was acquired under the pseudonym Jessie Murphy, for a Nazi retreat, from which Hitler would rule the US after his victory, and as a center from which to repopulate the US with Nazis. It was purchased by Norman and Winona Stephens, Nazi sympathizers, at the urging of Nazi spy Herr Schmidt. It had a barbed wire electric fence with vicious guard dogs. 50 Silver Shirts rallied and marched on the property. The day after Pearl Harbor, the FBI swept in and arrested everyone, also confiscating a short-wave radio that Schmidt used to contact his superiors. Schmidt later died in jail, and Norman and Winona were released.*

The story continues to evolve, but you will find most of the above nonsense repeated again and again.

As mentioned, Norman, his father, and his two oldest boys all played a role in supporting the US during World War II, with the two boys putting their lives on the line for our country. There is no evidence for the Nazi story, but someone had to be the first to start telling it. There is one document by a UCLA music professor named John Vincent, who was friends with Huntington Hartford, (who bought Murphy Ranch from the Stevens in 1949). He told the stories to Betty Lou Young, but she hesitated to print them without a more formal assertion that they were true. So, Vincent put his story down in the form of an affidavit in 1975, the text of which is:

=-=

AFFIDAVIT

In connection with the publication of a book that is being written by Betty Lou Young concerning the history of Rustic Canyon, in Los Angeles, California, I have furnished the following information:

I first became acquainted with the Murphy Ranch in 1948 when I was assisting Huntington Hartford with the selection and purchase of a site for the Huntington Hartford Foundation, later established on the Josepho and Murphy Ranch properties. The following information was derived from conversations with Winona and Norman Stephens--with their lawyer, Christian Hartke--and with Welton Becket, the architect who drew up the original plans for the installations at the Murphy Ranch. (Both Hartke and Becket are now deceased.)

When I first visited the Murphy Ranch, Winona and Norman Stephens were living in the steel garage, employing a caretaker to help maintain the extensive plantings. A guard was also employed who unlocked the gate to admit me. The entire property was surrounded by a chain link fence topped by barbed wire. A few people were present on the grounds. Goats, sheep, and cows were kept on the flatland at the bottom of the canyon. The Stephenses were eager to sell since they were having difficulties in trying to maintain such a large operation.

The facilities constructed on the ranch were part of a plan to establish a self-sufficient farm based on National Socialist ideals. Norman Stephens was a mining engineer with silver mining interests and his wife was the daughter of a wealthy Chicago industrialist who manufactured tacks. She had come to California with her mother and had an income from a trust. She was intrigued with metaphysical and supernatural phenomena and fell under the influence of a persuasive man named Schmidt who convinced her that he had superhuman powers. On one occasion, the Stephenses and Schmidt were driving in a car on a narrow, winding mountain road when they saw another car speeding toward them. As the car disappeared from sight beyond the curve ahead, Mr. Stephens expressed concern over meeting the car in such a hazardous place. Schmidt stated with conviction that the car would never reach them--and they did not see the car again after they rounded the bend.

Mrs. Stephens was so impressed with Schmidt that she believed implicitly in his warning that the end of the world was at hand. He advised them to build a protective wall and isolate themselves behind it, building a completely self-sufficient establishment where they and a select group could survive for at least a year and defend themselves if necessary. He convinced them that war was imminent, that Hitler's Germany was sure to defeat the United States, and that California would probably be destroyed in the process. Here in this mountain enclave, the chosen few would survive and, after the holocaust, emerge to repopulate the country.

The architectural firm of Wurdeman and Becket was engaged to draw up the plans. This was Welton Becket's first assignment after coming here from Washington State. He supervised the construction from a workshop on the project. A virtual Utopia was begun with its own water supply from springs, a double-generator power station as an alternative to the city power supply, and a 20,000-gallon fuel oil tank. Terraces were leveled and planted with trees, all supplied with copper pipes and a watering outlet for each tree. A culvert was built for the stream and a cold storage locker for storing food. The estimated cost of the improvements was four million dollars.

When war broke out, Schmidt was arrested for hiding short wave equipment on the property and sending messages to Germany. He died in prison before his case came to trial.

To my best knowledge and belief, the foregoing statements are true.

Signed in Los Angeles, California

Date: July 31, 1975

Signature of: Dr. John Vincent

Signature of witness: Thomas R. Young (ed. Randy Young)

=-=

This was written in 1975, 30 years after the Stevens family moved out of Murphy ranch in 1945. Vincent became involved with Murphy Ranch in 1948, as he says, working with Huntington Hartford on the purchase. So, everything he writes about the ranch before that date came from stories he heard. 27 years later, he wrote down what he believed from the stories. Maybe people were suspicious of the work being done there in the 30s, and in the general paranoia, they may have concocted stories that found their way to Vincent eventually. Note the odd confusion between Conrad Anderson and the mysterious "Herr Schmidt." There is a wanted poster for a Herr Schmidt from the era, but he was much younger than Anderson and didn't resemble him at all. And the poster was national, not focused on California.

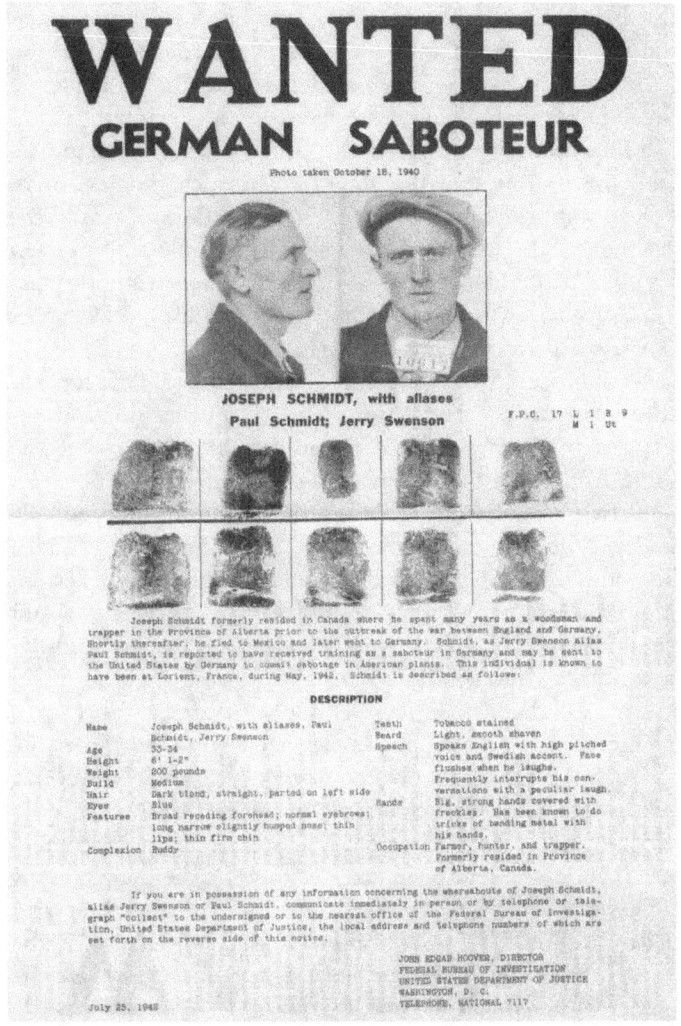

Herr Schmidt wanted poster. Photo: Special Collections and Archives, University Library, California State University, Northridge.

It is surprising that Vincent would get something so wrong regarding Norman and Winona living in a "garage" on the ranch in 1948. They moved from the ranch to Ramona in 1945. Winona never returned, but Norman visited often to keep everything from falling to ruin while trying to sell it. Carlile and Robin also visited to help maintain the place, up to 1949. That was one reason they were so "eager to sell." They sold it to Huntington Hartford for $100,000, despite having invested $900,000 in it. The statement he makes about four million dollars in improvements is way off, though it, like everything else, is quoted unquestioned in many articles.

The most frustratingly incorrect statement is, "The facilities constructed on the ranch were part of a plan based on National Socialist ideals." This one sentence underlies the entire urban legend, and despite no further evidence whatsoever, it has been believed every time the allegation is reprinted. Where did Vincent hear this? Certainly not from the Stevens (whose name he misspells "Stephens" throughout the document). The idea that Norman Stevens, who worked so hard on behalf of the US during the war, would say in 1948, "By the way, before the war we were Nazis" is ridiculous. Not even real Nazis would say that! More likely, the urban legend was already floating around at the time, and Vincent was just repeating it. Stories about Nazis pick up momentum on their own accord, with no facts necessary.

The statement about Norman's silver mining interests is also incorrect. There are many other inaccuracies. The water came from wells, not springs. There was no "select group" from which to "repopulate the country," it was just the family, Conrad Anderson, three of his older woman followers, and a changing set of one or two hired hands. Only Winona could have potentially borne children, but she turned 47 in 1940.

Much of what he writes about, especially descriptions of the ranch, is what everyone knew at the time and could easily verify. But his statements about the motives of the builders seem to be distorted versions of the real story, so are most likely passed along to him by others. Certainly, they can't be verified, and neither can the amazing claim that Herr Schmidt operated a short-wave radio connection to Germany and that he was arrested and died in prison! There is nothing at all to back up this part of the story, no newspaper records, no arrest of Conrad Anderson or Herr Schmidt, and even those who could check within the FBI's records have found nothing. The family all would have known if Conrad Anderson had been arrested, and he died while living on the ranch in 1943, years after the supposed FBI raid. Vincent seems to have been particularly gullible to have swallowed this tall tale. Yet the resulting urban legend survives with new articles propagating it all the time. The big mystery is where Vincent picked up this story.

I have posted my father's and uncle's affidavits about their experiences in Appendix B.

There are many articles about Murphy Ranch as part of Huntington Hartford's 1950s and 1960s artist colony. Famous writers lived there, such as Christopher Isherwood and Henry Miller, and there were many articles in the Los Angeles Times about the artist colony. Yet only one article refers to the Nazi legend, courtesy of John Vincent. He certainly liked to tell the story: in 1963 he told a Los Angeles Times reporter that the family had been convinced to build the ranch by a German spy. Nothing in any of Huntington Hartford's interesting history says anything about suspicious activities at Murphy Ranch before he owned it, or of any evidence found of something sinister.

Dozens of newspapers (including the LA Times), magazines, TV programs, and internet articles blithely repeat the stories almost weekly. It seems the only research they do is to read earlier stories and repeat them! No one at all, not even Randy Young, took the trouble to find the Stevens family, which wasn't hard to do. An amateur genealogist could do it easily, as was proved in the reader comments in a September 24, 2014, article in LA Curbed, entitled, *What Really Happened at Rustic Canyon's Rumored Nazi Ranch?* A commenter on the story, screen name "shmily," laid out the full names, and birth and death dates of Norman, Winona, and their parents, and named all their children. She did this with probably nothing more than membership in ancestry.com. This was a feat apparently beyond the LA Curbed author's journalistic skill, or of any of the authors of articles and sensational TV segments. After all, why do actual work on getting facts right when the article will already sell just because it mentions Nazis?

The articles continue to proliferate. The Wikipedia page I mentioned refers to a half dozen mostly solid-sounding publications like Slate, the Los Angeles Times, and the Huffington Post. But the person putting together the Wikipedia entry was not too discriminating in his sources. Some references contain extravagant embellishments, such as this quote included on the Wikipedia page: "On Monday, December 8, 1941, the day after the Japanese attack on Pearl Harbor, local police occupied the compound and detained members of the 50-strong caretaker force." This is a quote from an article in the U.K.'s Daily Mail, not exactly a bastion of good journalism. Half of the article is nonsense, not even quoting Randy Young correctly. Randy vehemently denies he ever said, "This was supposed to be the seat of American fascism from where Hitler would one day run the United States."

This is a new world where all kinds of information, ranging from malicious lies to the great truths of life, are on equal footing; they are available to all with no clear leadership in separating it for the people trying to make sense of it all. I'm sure someone is working on another rehash of the old story right now, perhaps for the History Channel again, or another installment for the Travel Channel. Will fascination with Nazis ever die out? Reading more and more of the nonsense, I realized I had a big challenge in trying to defeat this multi-headed hydra of a story. I could try to respond to and counteract each story, but when you cut a head from the hydra it grows two more. I can see new entries on blogs and websites almost every day, each repeating the same nonsense.

Some people have tried to find the Stevens and reached out to a family member. One contacted me, eager to confirm his elaborate suspicions. He informed me that he was "ready to announce that the origin of the Nazi influence was Winona's Stanford sorority." And if he had announced something so ridiculous, it would have ended up being quoted by someone! Yet when I mentioned this to another conspiracy theorist writing about the ranch, he dug up the fact that two of Winona's sorority sisters were daughters of a famous eugenicist. This must be what the first person found. I know it is not good to look at the world only through rose-colored glasses, but conspiracy theorists must have something awful smeared on their glasses, they see everything as evidence of a sinister plot.

Here is an exchange from the comments section of LA Curbed, where my aunt Toni (Theanne, Norman and Winona's youngest child) speaks up to correct the nonsense. It is the first time anyone from the family tried to do this in these forums.

=.=.=.=.=.=.=.=.=.=.=.=.=.=

Posted on Aug 30, 2015 | 5:00 PM
zorro
I am Norma Theanne Stevens, called Toni since I was 14. My dad, Norman Stevens, built this beautiful ranch, and we lived there during the war. Carlile (Steve) and I went to Santa Monica Canyon School near Sunset Blvd and the beach. All of this about nazis and a Herr Schmidt is a bunch of garbage, totally made up by some kook. Verna Weber was our teacher. We both went to Stanford as did my mother, Winona Basset. I am in my 80's and lived in Laurel Canyon for years. I have just lost my husband, Bud Pepper, and live in San Diego County. My mother died in '54, the year I graduated from Stanford.

Posted on Sep 10, 2015 | 5:00 PM
tlspam
@zorro: Well that isn't nearly as an entertainmenting of a story as a mysterious compound for Nazis. Let's keep spreading the silly idea that "Herr Schmidt" was preparing the way for Hitler!

Posted on Oct 2, 2015 | 5:00 PM
PayMeMoar
@zorro:

Hi Toni

The OSS intercepted secret communiques between Schmidt and Nazi officers in Mexico, South America and Europe and raided your parent's property and found a clandestine shortwave set. Records say your parents were taken into custody along with Schmidt. They were cleared and released while Schmidt later died in jail.

You are right though that the Ranch was never the Nazi headquarters some have suggested. That was Deutscher Haus in downtown Los Angeles which had according to a 1941 LA Examiner piece had 300 sworn Nazis.

=.=.=.=.=.=.=.=.=.=.=.=.=

Though the first reply to Toni recognizes the likelihood of it being an urban legend, it is amazing that the second commenter, someone who has swallowed the urban legend, thinks they can correct someone who had lived there! And with no facts, just repetition of the legend stated as if it were true. This person even added embellishments I've seen nowhere else about secret communiques!

It is impossible to prove a negative. Can anyone one hundred percent prove that their grandparents weren't Nazis? It is possible to prove someone is a Nazi, given clear evidence, but none has been provided in my grandparent's case.

It was clear to me that a letter to the editor of the LA Times was not going to be nearly enough to address the nonsense, even if they did print it and expose the mistakes that more than one of their reporters had made. I had to lay out the real story so that it is obviously much more likely to be true than the imaginative urban legend. That is one of the purposes of this book. The other is to give the people of Los Angeles the chance to get to know one of their most remarkable and influential individuals, Norman F. Stevens. He set his mark on the 20th century, and not in the way the urban legends tell. The last chapters of this book will tell that story.

9 HUXLEY, LEARY, AND ALPERT/RAM DASS

When I was a kid in the 1960s, I thought my grandfather Norman looked cool. He was a distinguished-looking old man with long white hair. He reminded me of Krishnamurti, whom we would sit on the grass and listen to in Ojai, California when visiting my grandmother. Norman would look at me with a sharply considering eye, like you might hope Gandalf would look at you and see something of merit. He was my father's father, and my first definite memory of him was his visit to my mother's mother when I was maybe nine years old. She said later, "I almost married that man." That would have been interesting! She had been a Broadway actress with several husbands along the way. I suppose it was possible.

Norman married Josephine Hogue in 1968 (Winona died in 1954). They would send us puzzling Christmas bulletins, with phrases like "The Christ is on the planet!" and "New Group of World Servers." My mother didn't try to explain them, just said he was a special person. My sister and I didn't know what to make of them at all. They sent us small gifts at Christmas. We did not know them very well as kids, beyond a few visits. But I do remember their two Siamese cats. They were very sleek, aware, and vocal. They made me think of the two troublemaking cats in the Disney movie. "The Lady and the Tramp."

Norman and Josephine   *Stevens Family Archives*

A friend and I drove down the West Coast in the summer after I graduated from high school, and we visited Norman and Josephine along the way. I remember her kindliness and her hoarse voice; she had problems with her throat over the years. They were smiling, friendly people, easy to like. Neither gave me any clue as to what they were up to with their spiritual pursuits. I heard later that Josephine had looked me over and determined I wasn't ready. I guess I wasn't!

Years later, I visited him on my own. My father had given me a copy of *The Rainbow Bridge*, which I read with wonder on my trip down the coast. A tear comes to my eye now, just as it did the moment Norman opened his door in San Marcos at the end of my trip down the coast, and I recognized him as my spiritual teacher. What many spend their whole lives searching for, I found at 21, in my grandfather. The impact on my life was vital to this day. When it comes to spiritual things, the world is full of confusion, ignorance, and nonsense, as well as deliberate lies. Norman and Josephine had spent their lives sorting it all out and separating the gold from the tons of rock. Looking for this core information in a New Age bookstore or on the internet is like searching for a needle in a haystack. I have been extremely fortunate, and very grateful for their help, and have tried to share what they gave me.

This is not to say that Norman was a perfect God-filled being. Anyone who thinks their human teacher has it all figured out and sets a perfect example in his/her thinking and behavior is making a serious mistake.

Norman was intensely aware of how much further he had to go and worked with incredible will on his progress while helping others. I got to know him as the human "student of the ancient wisdom" that he was and learned even a truly good person can make mistakes, and be worthy of love and respect, nonetheless. While I was his student, I made some big mistakes, too, and it is still hard to think I disappointed him.

One thing that affected the whole family was his continual insistence that there would be a worldwide economic collapse, and we should all get away from the big cities, store food and silver, and be part of a community where all would see each other through two years or so of chaos before civilization would be restored. I'm sure that Norman's concern about this was why he went along with the plan to build the survival retreat in Rustic Canyon in the 1930s (known now as Murphy Ranch). When I saw interest rates hit 18% in 1981, I thought he might be right, and started preparing. I asked my father about it. He said Norman had been predicting the same thing continually since the 1930s, and he (my father) had decided he could not live his life with the alarm bell ringing all the time, so he just carried on with business as usual.

It has been fascinating to read Norman's bulletins to his group over the years. They are mostly about the spiritual work, but there is also the repeated warning about an economic crisis, possibly precipitated by a natural disaster. However, after Josephine died in 1979, he told everyone about an experience where Josephine came to him and told him he could stop worrying about economic collapse, it was all going to be ok. He was very relieved and happy to tell the group. But after six months or so, the warnings started to creep back into the bulletins, probably due to the bad recession, inflation, and interest rates of the times, and they continued for the rest of his life.

Unfortunately, Josephine died before I had moved to California from the East Cost in 1980, so I never got to know her well. Over the last few years, I have been collecting family photos and letters, and now know her better through her correspondence with people, including Alice A. Bailey, the founder of the Lucis Trust and the Arcane School. Alice would assign some of the more difficult students to her, letting Josephine correspond with them to work through their challenges.

Josephine had some remarkable abilities, the rarest of which was to be able to objectively perceive a person's subtler energy bodies, sometimes called clairvoyance, which she and Norman made much use of in their research. At one point in the late 60s, they were visited by Timothy Leary and Richard Alpert, who hoped Josephine could tell them more about how the LSD they were taking was affecting them. They had found Josephine through Laura Huxley, wife of Aldous Huxley, both friends of Norman and Josephine's. She had a look at them and told them they were doing some damage to their nervous systems. It is not surprising that she found damage. Leary and Alpert were taking LSD like Linus Pauling took Vitamin C, all thinking they had found the ultimate thing to ingest.

Timothy Leary and Richard Alpert   *Wikimedia Commons*

Years later, a bearded man in a robe visited them. Josephine met him and said, "You are Alpert, aren't you?" even though he had been introduced as Ram Dass. He confirmed that he had taken a new name. I don't know if she knew what a leader he had become in the spiritual community. But he wanted her to have another look at him. She looked and reported that the damaged areas had been either healed or sealed off to cause no problems. Apparently, his teachers in India had helped him in this way.

Norman told me years later that Timothy Leary had never healed the damage, though I don't know if he knew this because Leary visited again. I saw Leary speak in the late 1970s and remember a roar of approval from my fellow Cornell University students when he started with "Let me say this first, before anything else: I am pro-drugs!" It was the seventies, after all. And Timothy Leary on drugs, what a part of the sixties!

As I mentioned, Aldous Huxley and his wife Laura were friends of Norman and Josephine, visiting them when they were living in Burbank. Huxley, the author of *Brave New World*, and *The Doors of Perception* was one of the few well-respected authors who dared to write about their personal experiences with psychedelic drugs. They met the Huxleys through Laura's friend Marjorie Hall, who was a member of the prototype group, and whose beautifully purified aura graces the back cover of the Rainbow Bridge books.

Norman told me once that he had always been a seeker, struggling to make sense of the purposes behind everything, and the nature of human life. He spoke of times when he felt he was in the dark about everything. One of these times he was in a library, wondering if any of the books contained truth he could recognize. He paced up and down the aisles. Suddenly a book held his gaze; he pulled it from the shelf. It was "The Secret Doctrine" by Helena P. Blavatsky, the founder of Theosophy; a book Albert Einstein supposedly always kept on his desk. This book started Norman in the direction he would follow for the rest of his life. But even in his early years things were different for him.

As a child in Maine in the 1890s, Norman had heard about angels from the Mormon missionaries. He and another boy made elaborate geometric patterns in the snow; he told me that the angels had guided them. He also told me that until his seventh year, he spent his nights in dreams of the torture chambers of the Spanish Inquisition, something left over from a previous incarnation. When he was 9 years old or so, he found Marie Corelli's book "A Romance of Two Worlds" in the attic. Marie Corelli wrote of higher worlds, advanced beings; the more loving and light-filled side of the supernatural. She was very popular in the late 1800s and was Queen Victoria's favorite author. Norman always remembered that book and often thought about the ideas in it.

His research continued all his life, even though the Second World War and family duties put it on hold at times. When he and Winona first got together, they practiced Christian Science. But when the children had moved out and the family fortune was nearly spent, he turned all his attention to his search for truth. Norman was determined, intelligent, and self-confident enough to contact anyone who seemed to have something interesting to say. At one point in the early 1950s, he heard about L. Ron Hubbard, a science fiction writer, and the founder of Scientology, and introduced himself to him. He was very intrigued, and for a while, Carlile and Theanne participated in early versions of "Dianetics" techniques as experiments. Norman told several of us that Hubbard had told him there was "no money in science fiction, the real money is in religion." That quote has been attributed to Hubbard by others, over the years, as well.

Eventually, he discovered the writings of Alice A. Bailey, about the esoteric knowledge of reality, and wore out three sets of the twenty volumes reading and researching. Norman met Josephine Hogue Leask in the 1960s, a fellow seeker. Josephine was one of Alice A. Bailey's secretaries for many years, handling correspondence with multiple individuals.

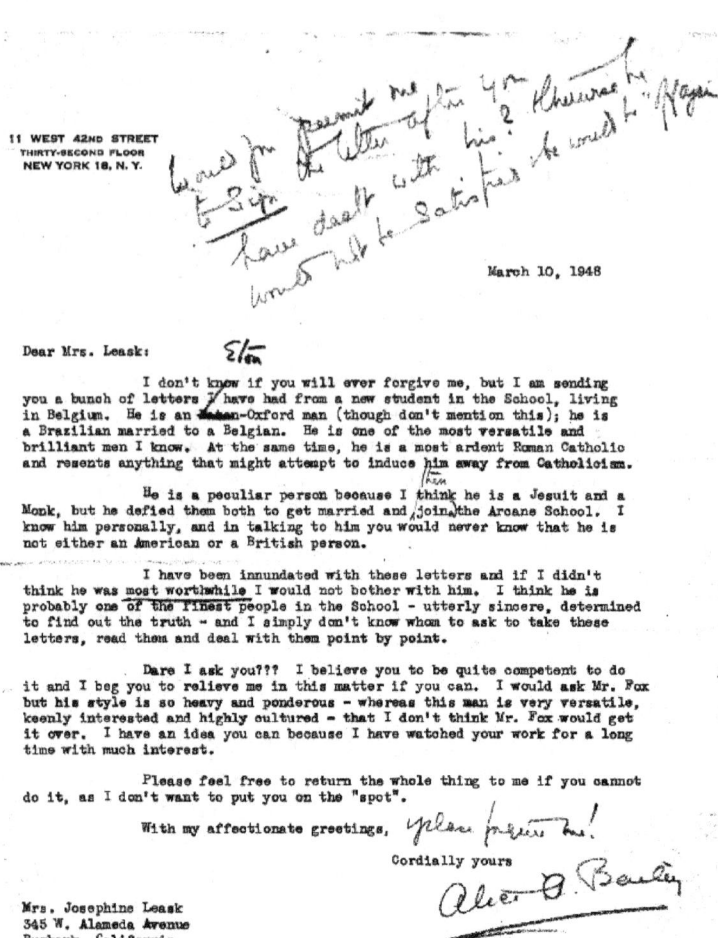

11 WEST 42ND STREET
THIRTY-SECOND FLOOR
NEW YORK 18, N. Y.

March 10, 1948

Dear Mrs. Leask:

I don't know if you will ever forgive me, but I am sending you a bunch of letters I have had from a new student in the School, living in Belgium. He is an Oxford man (though don't mention this); he is a Brazilian married to a Belgian. He is one of the most versatile and brilliant men I know. At the same time, he is a most ardent Roman Catholic and resents anything that might attempt to induce him away from Catholicism.

He is a peculiar person because I think he is a Jesuit and a Monk, but he defied them both to get married and join the Arcane School. I know him personally, and in talking to him you would never know that he is not either an American or a British person.

I have been innundated with these letters and if I didn't think he was most worthwhile I would not bother with him. I think he is probably one of the finest people in the School - utterly sincere, determined to find out the truth - and I simply don't know whom to ask to take these letters, read them and deal with them point by point.

Dare I ask you??? I believe you to be quite competent to do it and I beg you to relieve me in this matter if you can. I would ask Mr. Fox but his style is so heavy and ponderous - whereas this man is very versatile, keenly interested and highly cultured - that I don't think Mr. Fox would get it over. I have an idea you can because I have watched your work for a long time with much interest.

Please feel free to return the whole thing to me if you cannot do it, as I don't want to put you on the "spot".

With my affectionate greetings,

Cordially yours

Mrs. Josephine Leask
345 W. Alameda Avenue
Burbank, California

A Letter from Alice A. Bailey to Josephine Leask (name before marriage to Norman.) Stevens Family Archives

Norman and Winona were also friends of Alice and her husband Foster Bailey, and Norman served on the board of the Arcane School founded by Bailey for seven years. As I mentioned at the beginning of the book, Josephine had some special abilities, along the lines of what people call clairvoyance, which she didn't mention to many people, or Norman, right away. For a person of Norman's scientific yet spiritual orientation, these abilities were intriguing, especially if they could help with his research into the mysteries of life.

Norman read, researched, and meditated on the esoteric teachings as did others in those days, like a growing number of seekers do to this day. But he came to a conclusion that was not reached by most of the others. He was determined to use the information, do something with it, and take the next steps that went beyond anything in the books. I can tell you from experience, Norman was a person with an incredible will, unstoppable once set in motion. He was in perfect health in the 1960s; he was over 70 but age didn't slow him down or take the edge off him in any way. He did not smoke or drink his whole life. He studied martial arts and achieved an advanced level in judo at 70. He never had cancer, heart disease, or anything else more serious than a hernia or back pain throughout his one-hundred-year life. I'm sure good genes had a lot to do with it, and I am grateful to have been passed those genes. But I think his spiritual work played a big part, too. I am even more grateful that he passed that part of his life along to me and many others.

Josephine didn't initially tell Norman about her abilities, but he suspected them. The way he confirmed them was the beginning of the great project he and Josephine would do together, culminating in the creation of the Rainbow Bridge books. They were the "Two Disciples" listed as the authors of the books.

Norman investigated everything that came his way, and in the 1960s, a lot of new ideas, philosophies, and techniques were being circulated. He investigated Buddhism, Hinduism, and other Eastern teachings that were just beginning to get widespread attention in the West, as well as Masonry, in which he reported he achieved the highest degree. He also investigated new teachings forming alongside him in Southern California; the beginnings of Scientology, "Teachings of the Inner Christ," along with "New Thought" religious movements like "Science of Mind" and Unity.

But he ran into trouble when he tried some breathing exercises designed to open the *chakras*, energy centers of the body. As he tells it, the exercises worked far too well, opening energy flows into a body unprepared for it, energies that began by burning away anything that got in their way. He lost 30 pounds in a week and was sure he was dying. He went to Josephine and said, "I know you can see! What is happening to me? Help me!" She agreed to try to help Norman with his crisis. He reviewed all the techniques he had picked up over the years and tried them, while she observed the effects. He tried prayers, affirmations, mantras, and visualizations. She told him nothing was changing; his chakras were raging torrents of energy and he was still in serious trouble. She saw that it was not the energy or even its destructive effect that was the main problem. It was that the bodies, both physical and subtle, were not able to dispose quickly enough of the residue from the destruction of the subtle material structures being burned away. There is an old esoteric saying that helped them find the solution: "Energy follows thought." They finally saw an improvement when they visualized a six-foot-wide whirlwind of light forming over Norman's head, gradually moving down through his body, and then dropping deep down into the earth. As it moved through his body it picked up some of the excess residue material. Each time they passed this vortex, as they called it, through his body, more residue was carried into the earth. Norman's health recovered quickly.

They discovered something else which made the effort more effective. If Norman tried to identify with his higher self before visualizing the vortex, by saying, "I am the Soul," more energy immediately flowed into the vortex and it became much more effective, speeding up the process. Norman told me this identification with the Soul made every technique and effort much more effective. They made sure to include it in every spiritual exercise they did from that time forward. He told me once, "It doesn't matter if you are a holy roller, if you invoke the Soul, you will roll all that much better."

When I was learning about meditation from Norman years later (I was his student for years), he asked me what I did first when I sat down to meditate. I said, "I take a couple of deep breaths, try to get centered, left and right, front and back..." "No!" he said, interrupting me. "Always start with the Soul Mantram." This is a set of five lines, the first of which is, "I am the Soul."

Norman and Josephine gradually brought together a group of people who meditated with them and used the techniques they had developed. The techniques, among which were *identification with the Soul* and use of the *spiritual vortex*, as they called it, helped people in several ways. To Josephine, who was always aware of people's auras, most people looked like they were surrounded by thunderclouds of foggy, muddy-colored light. Norman, in the spirit of experimental science, took careful notes and drew diagrams of the changes Josephine saw in the subtle bodies of the group members. These showed the steady reduction of the cloudy, dark patterns, and brighter light shining out from within the person as obstacles to it were removed. These experiments, and the efforts with this group, which they called the *prototype group*, laid the groundwork for the Rainbow Bridge books, the first of which came out in 1975. These books were very popular among those who would become the first members of the New Age movement.

Norman and Josephine's teaching emphasized that Soul consciousness was collective among Souls and was the Christ consciousness properly realized. They wrote about the return of Christ, meaning the head of the spiritual hierarchy of beings in the next kingdom beyond human. They talked about laws of life such as Karma, or the law of sowing and reaping, and reincarnation.

Norman remembered some past lives and told me about one I was in. He was the head of a family of French nobility around the time of the French Revolution. I was one of his four sons, a priest. The revolution had begun, during the part of our lives he described. We were all gathered at the chateau prepared to escape the mobs. He had a detailed escape plan in place, with carriages and boats. But the old Aunt, whom he mentioned as a person he knew again in this life, refused to leave. So, we all stayed, were caught, and eventually guillotined. When visiting France years ago, I had a good laugh thinking of this story as I stood where the guillotine had been. There were the same buildings surrounding the square, and here was a new version of me. Chopping off my head was not as final a solution as they thought! French people have given me some important opportunities in this life, perhaps there is some karmic connection in that.

Norman spoke in detail about an incarnation where he came to California as part of the gold rush of 1849. He had a claim in Mariposa and remembered many aspects of the town and life back then. He did well, took his wealth to the Southern US, and set himself up as a plantation owner, with slaves. The last thing he remembered about that life was a barn full of wounded men, so he may have died in the Civil War.

He remembered something else: being kind to his slaves. He said the neighboring plantation owner was cruel to his slaves, however, and said to him, "The only thing they understand is the whip!" Norman said one day in this California lifetime there was a knock on his door, and he opened it to see the other plantation owner, easily recognizing him from the previous lifetime. But this time he was incarnated as a Black man!

During the time I knew him, he told me about some truly difficult, and sometimes funny, situations he faced as a spiritual teacher. In the 1960s and 1970s people were seeking gurus, and if they looked hard enough, some found him. He told me about one man who came to his door, very excited that he had at last found a true spiritual teacher. Norman's reply was, "Oh! Well, come in. Can I get you something to drink?" The man came in and talked and talked about the different approaches he had tried, books he had read, and teachers he had followed. All Norman got a chance to say was, "Is that so?" every so often.

Finally, after a couple of hours, the man became upset and said, "I don't think you have anything to say at all! I don't think you are a guru at all!"

"Well, I'm not a guru..." Norman replied.

The man cut him off, "Well you don't know anything at all, do you! So, I'm just wasting my time?"

"Well..." Norman replied.

"That's just great." The man stormed out of the house.

Fortunately, many others were willing to listen as well as talk. I remember visiting him and looking at each of the young people having lunch with him one day, suspecting them of special powers and abilities like something out of a Carlos Castaneda book. Years later, I remember standing up to talk to a group of older people who had been his students. I was surprised to see power and clarity in their eyes I hadn't expected. The Rainbow Bridge techniques are about clearing out the obstacles to love, light, and correct perception of reality, and they had been using the techniques for many years.

I also met one of his students who should never have studied the teachings. He had become convinced that he was central to the battle between good and evil on Earth and had lost his grip on reality. His life was full of imagined danger and challenges. Norman tried to help him, but the person was schizophrenic and locked in his delusions.

I remember visiting Norman in the 1970s and commenting on a poster he had: Christ, with his hands outstretched, was superimposed over a peace symbol, arms aligned with it. Radiating from behind the figure were fluorescent orange rays in a tight geometric pattern, with an almost stroboscopic effect. It was a dazzling piece of sixties art, and I had seen it before and have since in various places. It turns out he had created it! He was a good draftsman and had artistic skills.

Norman created this for Winona.   *Stevens Family Archives*

Norman taught me to meditate. I have had some beautiful times in my life and survived some bad times; meditation has helped with both. Eckhart Tolle says the influence of an awakened person on another is simple; it is like putting a burning log next to one that is not, soon both are burning. To be with someone who simply knows, who has no doubts whatsoever, and who states the esoteric facts again and again, as if they were the most obvious things in the world, is as inspiring as it is rare. It attracted many followers. I enjoyed taking him to meet with different groups of people up and down the West Coast. Every so often someone contacts me about meeting with him or being his student thirty or forty years ago and talks about how they still use the techniques he taught.

I was proud of my grandfather and honored to be the grandchild he eventually trusted to carry on the printing of his books. I never had an attraction to spiritual gurus; I'm not the devotional type. But when I saw how he greeted every new person with a welcoming smile, and shared whatever he could with them of his knowledge, wanting nothing from them but their questions, I felt he had gotten the same message as I had from the 60's – we are all brothers and sisters, and every attempt we make to love and respect each other is well chosen. He and I were alike in some ways; we both had a scientific and engineering background and wanted clear and specific information, not vague philosophies with Sanskrit words we would not be able to share even if we understood them.

Josephine died in 1979. Norman moved in with his son Dale for a while, and then in the mid-1980s, a spiritual community in Sweden at Stjarnsund invited him to come to live with them. The community was based on the Findhorn model. Families grew produce, and they had ceremonies together for the solstices and other holidays. Spiritual "tourists" would come up from Stockholm and join them for the ceremonies, this helped provide income. They welcomed him as a sort of "prophet from over the sea."

I, along with my first wife Colleen, and our year-old daughter Alia, visited him there over Christmas 1991. I remember the cold, clear, and very long nights; Stjarnsund is a two-and-a-half-hour drive northwest of Stockholm. There were some happy ceremonies; I remember walking in a circle in the snow and singing around a big Christmas tree with twenty or so other people. We were there for Norman's birthday on December 21, when he turned 99. Though the people there took great care of Norman, especially Erik Ahrberg, who had invited him, they thought he needed the care of his family at his age. So, we arranged that he would come live with us in Santa Cruz, California in March 1992.

I was making a long daily commute to the first major job of my software engineering career, and Colleen had her hands full taking care of the basic needs of a 1-year-old and a 99-year-old. Norman liked the food, but he hadn't stuck around all these years to eat nice meals and hang out playing the grandparent role. What he cared about was his spiritual work, and he was disappointed that we couldn't drive him up and down the West Coast to meet with people. After six months, he announced that he was returning to Sweden, would we please buy him an airplane ticket? I hesitated since he hadn't asked the people at Stjarnsund about it. But, as he somewhat angrily pointed out, I had no right to decide where he should be or where he should go, so we bought him a ticket, warned them that he was coming, and back he went.

They did take him in again, and two weeks before he died in February 1993, at 100 years of age, he spoke to a crowd of two hundred people in Stockholm. Back in Stjarnsund, he fell and broke a hip while on a chair trying to change a lightbulb. He went downhill quickly. He couldn't see well, had become very hard of hearing, and couldn't walk far. He must have been relieved to get out of that old body. He stayed in his body for so long because there were so few like him who could speak with such certainty about esoteric spiritual things; he knew that in times when everything was in question, he was desperately needed. And he had the incredible willpower to manage it. He was one stubborn old guy to hang in there to 100 years of age. I'm sure glad he did, and I am happy he can be free again, too.

The first Rainbow Bridge book was well received in what was to become the New Age community in 1975. It was reprinted several times, at 10,000 copies per reprint. Though I had been corresponding with my grandfather for years as his student, I had no idea about this popularity, thinking it was just family and friends who participated. One day in 1980, shortly after I had moved to Santa Cruz, California, a poster in the downtown bookstore caught my eye; the text was framed in a lovely rainbow. To my great surprise, it announced that a Rainbow Bridge meditation group was forming and mentioned the book! The book contains instructions for group meditations, and for selecting group members. Groups had formed all over the country based on it, and I was about to join one in Santa Cruz.

Meditations I had learned from Norman and done on my own had given me powerful experiences confirming I was on the right track with the Rainbow Bridge work and its emphasis on connection with the Soul. But group meditations proved to be even more powerful. It seems that the variety of energies of the individuals in a group can end up balancing out to produce something stable which provides what each person needs. People who approach each other with goodwill, intelligence, and open minds can work together to create something much greater than "the sum of the parts." I met unforgettable people in this group and shared experiences with them which deserve a book of their own. It was the first of many Rainbow Bridge groups I have joined or started over the years. The benefit to the individuals is only one aspect, the main purpose of the group is to bring through energies that assist humanity in its struggle to free itself from fear and ignorance, and to experience the love and joy that is humanity's destiny.

Norman and Josephine set to work on the second Rainbow Bridge book, released in 1982, called *Rainbow Bridge – Phase II – Purification*. It has remarkably powerful techniques for clearing the deep-seated thought patterns that condition our lives. It has now been reprinted several times. Unfortunately, both books are out of print now, but used copies can be found online. There is a plan to put them in a public online library so that all can read it free of charge. This will be announced on http://murphyranch.org.

Stanton K. Stevens

10 THE ONGOING STORY

There are so many interesting stories in our family, I can only touch on them here. I will keep expanding on them on the website. For instance, Norman's father, Ferdinand Stevens, was a famous balloonist in the early 1900s, entertaining crowds of 30,000 with daredevil stunts. Towards the end of this early career, before he decided to move on to a safer livelihood, he would climb into a cannon attached to a hot air balloon, and once aloft, he would be shot out and parachute to earth!

His "safer" second career was to become a liquor agent, and eventually sheriff of Androscoggin County, Maine. He was beloved by the local newspapers because of one exciting adventure and arrest after another. He ended his days living in Ramona with Norman and Winona and died in 1950. Some of the newspaper articles are posted on this book's website, https://murphyranch.org.

My father, Carlile (Steve) Stevens, was an inventor, holding more than 50 patents. He invented the solid-state fluorescent light ballast in the early 80s, which would have gone a long way to reducing our country's oil consumption, since it used half as much electricity as the technology in use at that time. But corporate shortsightedness and greed intervened. A large lighting corporation licensed his invention, but instead of making the billions with it that were possible, they put it on the shelf to be sure that no one, such as the Koreans, found out there was a better way that competed with the industrial method they were already using. Steve had to fight them in court for twelve years. Finally, he and his partners won a 96-million-dollar lawsuit against the corporation.

My Uncle Robin put tremendous creativity to work in creating amusements such as *The Disconnected Lady*. Traveling to county fairs and other venues, this exhibit showed a head connected via an actual heart-lung machine (they somehow got it surplus) to a body by many tubes. Nurses and doctors were allowed in for free! It was done with mirrors and lots of help from my cousins behind the scenes. He also taught high school drama and produced many plays. It feels wrong to summarize a fascinating life in a short paragraph. I will be adding much more to the website about Aunt Toni, Norman and Winona's parents, and their adventures, as time goes by.

Regarding the ugly urban legend: There are mysteries still to be solved, but one which should now be put to rest is whether the Stevens family would ever have had anything to do with Nazis. We hope this book will close the door to that long-running fiction. Readers, we would appreciate your help! The next time you see some blog repeating the old nonsense, point out the true story told in this book. My grandfather and uncles who fought for this country deserve better. Thank you in advance!

The End

APPENDIX A

After our trip to Murphy Ranch, I asked family members to write up their impressions. My cousin Carolyn's moving and eloquent story is below.

=.=

A TRIP TO THE RANCH

"Oh, my God. Holy crap. Oh, my God. Holy crap. Oh, my God. Holy crap!" As I jumped into my van to follow my cousin's rented SUV down the twisting streets of Malibu, I couldn't control my thoughts. My more articulate vocabulary chased me down the mountain, unable to catch up to conquer the looping stream in my mind. "Oh, my God. Holy Crap......" These aren't even words I typically say. "Oh, my God. Hoooleeee crap!"

A few months ago, I had no inkling of the adventure my cousin would deliver to my doorstep. Being bombarded with sales calls, I didn't answer his call after not recognizing his out-of-state number. His voice on the message was instantly recognizable, even though it had been at least a decade since we last spoke. The family lilt crooning over the phone, just a few tones to the left of my brother. He spoke of bringing my dad out for a visit. Ding. Red flag #1. We don't do family visits. Reunions. Get-togethers. Hangs. Not without a purpose. Someone is getting married. Or worse. He added that he is bringing his dad out too. Ding. Ding. Red flag #2. Additional guests to solidify that the visit will clearly be an event. He asked for dates and times that I would be available. I have to be honest, I listened to these dates with only a vague interest as I impatiently waited for the real reason behind the call. Dang. When did I become such a cynic? The phone call was ending. "It'll be great to see you," he quipped. Nice. I was wrong. Just a visit. Then just as he was hanging up, he tossed in, "And we can clear up all this Nazi business to set the family record straight." Click. Wait. What? I listened again. Yep. Nazi business. I laughed out loud. Which might seem like an odd response. However, what would constitute odd to most people is just a launching point for my family. In my family... odd is relevant. So I did what I always do when I need to bounce crazy off a sane wall. I called my brother. The center of information for the family. I can count on him for the facts. And we can count on each other to stroll through crazy town until we can label outrageous as creative. He confirmed the story. Nazi business. In my family.

I knew that my parents both grew up surrounded by wealth and affluence beyond my experience. I knew that during his formative years as a boy and teenager, my father was forced to live on land overlooking Malibu. Wait.

Forced? Yes. Forced. Because despite being insanely rich during the Depression. Despite having the resources to purchase prime real estate in Pasadena. Despite having forty-five acres in the hills of Topanga Canyon. Despite affluence, influence, and common sense, my father's parents were certain the world was going to end. Any minute. To their credit, doomsday was not an uncommon concept during WWII. Doomsday is not an uncommon concept today. And I have to hand it to them. They got behind their beliefs. Most people spout beliefs as criticisms to those who don't agree. Not my doomsday-predicting ancestors. They were private people. They didn't rally for support. They didn't shout it from the mountain tops. They didn't need validation from anyone. They just prepared. Quietly. Passionately. With ingenuity. They bought the land in Topanga to live, unassisted, for as long as the world would let them. They bought the property in the '30s but didn't move the family to the grounds until the '40s. They didn't try to save the world. They didn't hire people to help them manage the place. They built it for the family. To toil and hide. And toil they did. The kids were taught to farm the land and grow crops, something that I have always found somewhat amusing. Farming beachfront land in Topanga Canyon. It's always seemed a bit comical to me. Until today.

My cousin can expound on the details of what brought us to this day, this moment, this second, this breath in time. I am only here to gasp it in and share the exhale. I have many wacky stories from my childhood. My father is a creative genius who was somehow able to make a living dressing like a cat and singing karaoke tunes well into his seventies. But I digress...Today all the wacky stories from my life were dwarfed by the history of his upbringing. As we drove through the graffiti-ladened gates of his childhood home, I could see his hands shaking. And he doesn't shake. His breath was unsteady as, in barely a whisper, I heard him say, "I don't know about this." What started as an adventure to clear the family name was suddenly an uneven hike down memory lane. I put my hand on his, already choking back waves of emotion threatening to scream into the packed SUV. The park ranger greeted us, his face flushed with excitement. "Mr. Stevens?" he asked. Four men in the car answered, "That's us." The day before, there had been eight Mr. Stevens together as my dad and uncle prepared for this adventure with my two cousins, two brothers, and three nephews. All of these Stevens men. And none of them Nazis.

We followed the county and city jeeps onto the property. Immediately, my dad and his brother began chattering, pointing at tiny little details and expounding things like, "That's where you use the key to open the gate...this is the route to school...that's where the nanny stood when she wanted to yell at us..." Each man validating the other's memory. It was quickly easy to imagine them as boys, running through the trees and racing up and down the thousands of stairs that still remain on the property, connecting one "hill" to the next. It all seemed like one big lot to me, but as we wound around, they could easily identify which hill we were on. Never once were they confused. Never once did they doubt. They both knew every inch of the property, even though it had been almost seventy years since they had last been there. We spent the next few hours exploring the three hundred-thousand-gallon water tank, the one hundred-thousand-gallon fuel tank, the powerhouse, the small home of Conrad Anderson, a villain to be maimed later, greenhouses, gardens, curbs poking through bushes, and a multitude of nooks and crannies, each bringing a wealth of stories, memories, and emotions. Now and again, I would see my uncle pause from his usual joyful countenance to allow small waves of history to wash over him. Every ounce of anything standing was covered in graffiti, courtesy of the Nazi story. Hatred of the Nazis inspiring urban decay. And there is a different design every day. I'd like to think of it as a work in progress.

The Park Rangers were like kids on Christmas. Their love for the land was palpable. And their disgust at its demise was heartbreaking. My uncle's memory and knowledge of every detail was astounding. He pieced the puzzle together for them, identifying every ruin. He explained every stair and rod. He pointed to the beds crammed underneath the fuel house, noting that he and his siblings would sleep there so they could be available to monitor the power. He clearly had a lot to do with the operation of the "farm." The rangers were so sweet, eager to listen, and quick to normalize this outrageous survivalist camp with tales of their own families' attempts at packing extra food and keeping war rations just in case. I pondered these tales, leaning against the hundred-thousand-gallon water tank standing over thirty feet tall. At one point, I stood with my cousin behind the powerhouse, looking at the massive fuel tank. My cousin's new, beautiful wife was at my side, perhaps wondering what sort of crazy she married into. We looked around at the absolutely gorgeous day and marveled at our grandparents' inability to see the beauty. They were so busy preparing for the world to end, they never reveled in the beginning. They couldn't just... stop. And play in the canyons of Topanga. There was no 'now,' there was only the threat of no tomorrow. Not long after absorbing that profound realization, I stood in the main house, surrounded by appliances from the WWII era, or what was left of them. Everything was rusted and tossed aside. The dishwasher was an odd color and laid on its side, almost as though placed by a film crew. "Maybe it is all a hoax and Ashton Kutcher is going to come galloping down the mountain," I mused. Or maybe I am going to stand in the rusty dirt and take in the broken, battered, filthy, tagged remnants of my daddy's home. Maybe I am going to be overwhelmed by the massive amount of pain that still lingers until I feel hot tears spill down my cheeks. This was not a happy family on this beautiful land. They had the best that money could buy. The ruins still stand because they were made with the finest materials by the most skilled of hands.

I had watched a few hiking videos before coming on this trip. I had to turn them off because I couldn't bear to see hiking home videos narrated by uninformed "tour guides" repeating lies about the hundreds of people that were supposedly made to be slaves on this land. Pointing out my uncle's bed as being the dungeon of doom. Commenting on the eerie, dark, evil that lurks within as if they know. As if they were there. As if they were the descendants of the people that lived here. As if they were me. I honestly don't know my grandparents' political views. I know my father is far from racist. I have never once heard him express a racial slur, even as a joke. I would think if his parents were building a haven for Hitler, he might display traces of hate. I've never seen it. On him or his siblings. There has been a lot of crazy in this family... but I can safely say it is born of a nature that is too oblivious to be political. My grandfather was an engineer that created wings for fighter pilots. My dad was a Merchant Marine and my uncle served in WWII. There was a great deal of sadness permeating from these hills, but I can safely say Hitler kept his own personal sadness to his country. There was no one waiting to house him in California. At least no one in my family.

I have to admit when I first heard that a blogger was busy defacing my family's history, I had little interest. A blogger? So what. He is just repeating what his mother told him. She is just repeating what the uninformed neighbors decided must be true when they weren't invited onto the property. But as I watched my uncle describe the irrigation system that he designed and built with his own hands, as my father steered me away from poison oak, as the park rangers ran to and fro, finally getting answers to questions about the property that had been haunting them for decades, suddenly it all mattered. This wasn't ancient history. This was my history. My dad was here as a child, day after day, dreaming of what his life would become. My grandmother would have a heart attack on this very land, toiling it until it toiled her. She survived but, from what I understand, it was one of the reasons they finally left to buy a hundred acres of land in Ramona. Yep, they handed over the beachfront property to an artist colony and relocated to the land of chicken ranches, in another wacky story to be saved for another distant day. But today, with the sun pounding on my back, the smell of the ocean wafting through the air, and the sound of my father's whisper, telling story after story... today I was interested.

If you look at a map of the Topanga State Park, you will see a speck, off to the side, that is still owned by the County of Los Angeles. There it is. My family's legacy. It's going to take a fair amount of money to remove my father's home. And no one wants to pay. And so it sits, providing an ongoing canvas for creepy crawly artists. I had learned to find it comical that my inheritance was squandered on a dream. We are always told to follow our dreams. I am a firm believer in dreaming. And as devastating as it feels today...there is a large amount of awe that can be accessed when one considers the energy and commitment this family put into their dream. We always hear stories of people that refused to quit despite the odds. We hear stories of inventors that were called crazy because they wouldn't back down or listen to common sense. And we marvel at how the world has benefitted because of these dreamers. We encourage our children to think big and blaze a trail. We idolize, write books, make movies, spin You Tubes, and constantly remind each other of the big dreamers that created and refused to quit in spite of setbacks, failures, and losses. But what of the throes of dreamers that never quite learned from their failures? What of the creative folks that instead launched into the next big thing full of new hope and promise? We don't hear of their attempts. I wonder. How many more are out there? Full of passion and purpose, however misguided. The least we can do, my cousins and I, is tell their story. The least we can do is share a walk down memory lane…or a dirty trail in this case. A glimpse into one day amongst the many that were spent here. So much more to tell. But, for now, we'll just take in a trip to the ranch. For now, that is plenty!

Carolyn Stevens Carpenter

=-

My brother Todd Stevens also wrote up his observations and thoughts about the initial trip to the ranch with Randy Young, and on the trip with the rangers that Carolyn wrote about.

=-

It's odd. The canyon. Dad's stories taking on three dimensions. It's like watching a movie of a book you loved, and now there are faces put to the characters. Or rather, crumbled buildings put to the memories of those days, now trying to place the stories on the property as we walk. It's a step back in time, relics of our family's past vision. To enter the canyon, we walk through an extraordinarily rich neighborhood with pillared manors, spotless asphalt streets, and perfect grass-edge concrete curbs.

Within the first five minutes, we're past the outlying boundaries of the Palisade estates. Abruptly, the landscape shifts as we enter the edge of the wilderness beyond.

Our guide, Randy, tells us wild stories we know to be untrue (we divulge to him who we are before day's end). We move past the last remnant of more modern dwellings: an abandoned house perched on the edge of the narrowing canyon mouth, fenced with barbed wire, windows and doors boarded up. The perfect asphalt and concrete give way to spans of rutted dirt road. On the left is a steep drop into the canyon, on the right side is dirt, dry grass, and rock faces on less steep hillsides. Our guide goes on with stories he's told so many times in the last thirty years. It's difficult not to chuckle at the fascinating fabrications. Fire is a part of this landscape. I see the scars uphill from our path, which shifts again to a well-maintained asphalt fire road. We walk around the locked gate as other hikers zigzag around the other side. Early sightseers, already returning before this 90-degree day becomes too uncomfortable, heading back toward the money-green landscapes. Twenty minutes in, we reach the corner of the canyon ranch. It is marked by a steel pole, wrapped by cyclone fencing, topped with a finial. The fence and racks of barbed wire along the top look less than a decade ago, not showing much of the age of the last seventy-five years.

After a few more steps, our guide pauses at the top of a flight of concrete stairs. Only we know the name of this set of stairs: Number 1. It is one of ten staircases that scale the canyon sides. Our guide reveals his reverence for the stairways, as he shares about their profusion and the marvel of labor that went into their creation. I agree. My back hurts, imagining the effort.

We begin. I'm charged with video documentation, and dance ahead of our small contingent, single file down the staircase. I alternate between sideways stepping and straight ahead, panning the camera back and forward. The steps are shallow and drop steeply, though galvanized pipe handrails to each side are there if I miss a step. Randy reminds me about rattlesnakes; I decide the camera can watch the three behind me, and I'll look ahead.

It seems the staircase has no end. We've been walking for five minutes, and it trails down, disappearing as it twists slightly into the dense thicket which surrounds us like a tunnel. This path is a welcome relief from the sun, but my construction-worn knees are complaining. I'm thankful when we finally step off the five-hundredth and something step, ending at a roadway that's in bad shape. We have crossed into tagger territory now. Any bit of man-made surface—retaining walls, water and fuel towers, relic structures—all are targets for graffiti artists.

Some of the art is fair. All of it is colorful, a marked contrast to the light grays and greens of the trees in this dry valley. It does not make a negative impression on me; I have no attachment that this place should be anything other than what it is now. But I know the stories. I try to imagine the valley as private, secured with fences and locked gates. The sound of the cicadas would have been drowned out by the generators which rumbled night and day, providing all the power to pump vast wells, run acres of irrigation and light the staircases and houses. It's peaceful now. Lots of birds... and voices—this is a city park now, open to hikers and elusive painters.

We come first to the generator building. It's the only building on the property still standing. Its walls are eight-inch-thick concrete. We use our feet to sweep through a small sea of discarded spray paint cans and step up the front stairs. The powerful aerosol smell greets us. Through the open doorway, we see an incredible angel is there to make up for the offense. It seems impossible some kid, with cans of white and black could have created the fine detail in this masterpiece of passing art.

I look around at the rest of the murals. Directly above the angel is another face by a skilled artist, but the rest, covering every square inch, is mediocre, only joyous in the riot of color, and otherwise meaningless except to the individual or band of sprayers.

The angel seems to give grace to the setting; like entering a quiet church. I imagined it would also touch the hearts and minds of the circulating hoodlums, who passed by us occasionally on our foray, their backpacks rattling guiltily. But they are hoodlums indeed—by the time of our next visit, one day later, the angel had already been defiled. And after two days, she was gone, buried by slow-minded, desperate souls whose only design for recognition in this world is to write their name large and with style.

Everything in the canyon was done on a grand scale, and in the brief span of seventy-five years, nature had slapped those efforts down. The fire raging in '78 made rubble of two of the houses: one stucco, the other steel; it thoroughly burned a third house, two barns, and the rabbitry, leaving no traces. Rangy trees, referred to as big weeds by my father's brother, Robin, had grown up since then. They colonized the cleared bottomland of the canyon and subsequently dumped enough foliage over two-and-a-half decades to fill the 6-foot wide, 6-foot-deep concrete trench, which ran the length of the valley. The seasonal creek, forced out of that well-behaved waterway, had further cut up the landscape, moving soil to higher and lower levels and eroding banked hills to the point of minor landslides. When the "two gents," as the rangers called them, our father and uncle, came to see the property, it was nearly unrecognizable to them.

We spent three hours there with Randy, our historian-guide. Then it was time to tell him who we were. This was a moment of truth for us all. It had been the subject of debate how to handle the delicate denial of the many stories and rumors which had grown for over thirty years. Stanton handled it with great tact, and I watched Randy for his reaction. At first, it seemed there was not much, his character is calm and focused. But as the facts Stanton presented sank in, and he realized he might meet two people who had lived here, Randy told us the hairs on his neck were on end.

The next day, our family contingent: I, my brother, our father, our father's brother, his daughter (our cousin), and my brother's wife, we all descended on the ranch with the help of a 4-wheel drive. Stanton had made many calls to set this up, and state park rangers met us to unlock the gate so we could drive the seniors all the way down. City officials who had been overseeing the clearing of brush and other maintenance of the land also joined this foray. During our tour, several police officers and other rangers showed up, apparently all there to see the *actual* children of the couple who had built this compound, two people at the heart of the popular rumors which had brought it so much negative attention (and graffiti) over the last twenty-five to thirty years.

They treated our father and uncle with great affection and care as they listened to the truth of what this place had been so long ago. The elders reveled in the limelight (a familiar experience to them, one that they had shared in the days after they left the ranch forever—a story for the autobiography: *C.R. Stevens – The Two-Million-Volt Man*). An air of celebration accompanied the gathering, and it attracted the curiosity of hikers who happened by, wanting to know what was what. After we filled them in, we pressed the girls into service as amateur photographers. The family members, rangers, and officials passed camera phone after camera phone to the two girls and mugged for snapshots with the two celebrities of the moment.

The last day before departure from LA, Randy came to the Air BnB house to meet Steve (C.R. Stevens) and Uncle Robin. Randy was excited for the meeting, and Robin was deeply moved that Randy was on our side—or at least the side of the truth—and that he was committed to helping clear the family name of any connection to the Nazi rumors. New information went back and forth on that day, some of it revelatory, some of it mysterious, presenting more questions needing answers.

And that is what this book is all about!

=.-=.-=.-=.-=.-=.-=.-=.-=.-=.-=.-=.-=.-=.-=.-=.-=.-=.

My father, Carlile (Steve) Stevens also wrote up some observations from his trip.

=.-=.-=.-=.-=.-=.-=.-=.-=.-=.-=.-=.-=.-=.-=.-=.-=.-=.

My 70-year reaction to my return to the Canyon by Carlile R. Stevens

My first thought was the road in was in worse shape than when we lived there. I expected that after 70 years the road would go through and there would be houses on it. It still is the only way in or out, much to my surprise.

The main gates looked like they always did. We stopped at the concrete tank and the lid was gone, which I expected from Google views. What surprised me most was that I expected everything to look much smaller, as I was small when I lived there, so everything was big to me then. I thought that, since I was now much bigger, everything would seem relatively smaller. It did not. The concrete tank, as well as other things, looked just as big as it did 70 years ago and much deeper now that it was empty.

My next shock was the amount of overgrowth. We had always kept the property clean and manicured. The weeds had turned into trees over our heads and over the road in many places. The nice, paved road was now rutted and washed out in many places. We went by the new road to Josepho's, which had not been there before, and on to the upper dump, which looked much the same.

We stopped the car at the Upper House, where Conrad Anderson lived and died. It was mostly gone with one tree growing through what used to be the washing machine. There was so much growth it was hard to define the foundation. I identified a wall to the garage where I used to go to take care of Blackie and Brownie when they were puppies.

We continued down the road past Chime Hill (Stair No.8) but I was not able to identify the road out to where the gazebo used to be. The big open canyon on the opposite side of the road from Chime Hill was also not to be identified due to the under and overgrowth. I understand the whole Chime Hill structure was destroyed in the fire in 1978 and is now so grown up that you can't even find the road that went out and around it. As we continued, we caught glimpses of staircases No. 1 and No. 2 but could not identify No. 3, the stairs I always used. We went by the lower dump across from the area where the main house was to be built, and past the road that led up to the greenhouses, which are now only foundations. We stopped at the Power House.

The Power House is more visible now as the big hedge of oleanders that used to be in front of it is gone. It was covered with graffiti, some of it pretty artistic. The generators and big engines that drove them were gone along with the big switchboard. The water coolant pumps, air compressors, pressure tanks, and coolant tanks were all gone. We were told by the rangers that the engines and generators were shipped to South America and were powering a small village, but Randy Young said that was not so. He said the engines were broken into small pieces and hauled away for scrap and he has one of the pistons. The 20K gallon diesel tank behind the Power House was melted and shrunk from the fire. I told the rangers about the lube oil tank buried on the hill above it. They did not know about it. Neither did Randy Young. The main control panel for the sprinklers is now just a piece of pipe sticking out of the ground. There is a fortune of copper pipe buried in the terraced hillsides.

Randy Young says he has pictures of everything before the fire. He has been at this for some time. Across from the Power House, there was a road that went across the ditch (the 6-foot-deep water channel) to the vegetable garden and root cellar. No sign of it now as the bottom land where we grew alfalfa is all ruts and washes from flooding. There was also a lower house next to it. I cannot see even a foundation for it. Randy says he has pictures of it.

While everyone was talking to the rangers at the Power House, Todd and I walked on to the main house, of which only the lower floor is still standing. It was a metal house, so the fire did not totally destroy it. I showed Todd where I thought stuff had been buried. The road past the main house that led to the barns and manure pits was no longer there past the incinerator due to washout and landslide from the bottom of No. 9. Could not see the No. 9 stairs but the No. 10 stairs along the North property line are still there and intact. Working through the brush, we did find the concrete wall of the manure pits. But we could get no further to the barns and pump house. Todd did find his way over to the ditch at just one place. We were unable to locate the duck pond or hen house. We spent some time trying to find our way around the bottom land with not much luck.

We then climbed back up to the main house. I identified the main house septic tanks for the rangers. They thought they were cisterns or part of an underground tunnel system. We told them there never was a tunnel system. I think they felt kind of dumb when they realized that, of course, there had to be a septic system. I had not realized how strong the main house was. The walls were heavy steel beams and plates, and the upper floor walls were still intact after the fire but laying on their sides or propped up by pieces of junk by the still vertical first-story walls.

We spent a lot of time with the rangers who invited us back any time. We answered lots of questions. We showed them where the underground gas tanks were and where the pump had been located.

It is hard to say how I felt and feel about all of this. There is some closure, but not much. There is certainly disappointment in seeing so much destruction and decay. What I remember has not changed much but my vision, when I think about the canyon, now has two images.

APPENDIX B

Both Carlile and Robin Stevens have signed affidavits stating their own recollections. Here is the text of the affidavits.

AFFIDAVIT – Carlile Stevens
In connection with the history of Murphy Ranch in Rustic Canyon in Los Angeles, California, and the Stevens family that built it and lived there, I am furnishing the following information:

My name is Carlile Richmond Stevens, the son of Norman and Winona Stevens (not Stephens). I lived at Murphy Ranch during the Second World War, from November 25, 1942, through July 1945. When I moved there the residents were: Norman Stevens, Winona Stevens, my sister Theanne Stevens, Josephine Spotts, Ilsa Reynolds, Conrad Anderson, and Florence Kamp. Hired hands came and went.

Contrary to any urban legends about Nazis and Murphy Ranch, the entire time I was there I never saw anything related to Nazis or National Socialism. There were no guards, guard dogs, marches, gatherings, or Nazi insignias. There was no one speaking German, and there was no discussion of Nazis beyond what would be normal during World War II. There was no one named Schmidt there or ever discussed. There was more concern about the Japanese, who could attack the West Coast, than the Germans.

Conrad Anderson, who was a spiritual healer, lived in his own separate house and was already living there when we moved in. All the rest of us lived in a building of about 3000 square feet, with 7 bedrooms, other rooms, and a 4-car garage. This is labeled "servant's quarters" on the architectural drawings, and was the main building on the property, with the intention that more would be built.

Approximately $900,000 was spent to build out Murphy Ranch from 1932 through 1942. My mother, Winona, provided the money, which came from my grandfather Arthur Bassett, who had made a fortune developing the round nail in Chicago. The property was purchased from Jessie Murphy, who my parents and sister met with a number of times. The ranch was intended to be entirely self-sufficient. Only a phone line connected it to the outside world; the power came from generators and the water from wells.

I operated all of the machinery, and knew it better than anyone there, even at my age.

My parents were strongly influenced by Conrad Anderson, who had healed Robin when he was very young and close to death when doctors and others had been unable to help. Anderson ran Murphy Ranch. Josephine Spotts and Ilsa Reynolds were wealthy followers of his who had given him their money. My parents were fascinated by his healing powers and predictions about the war and wanted to be safe whatever the outcome was. Anderson convinced them that they would be safe if they built their self-sufficient retreat. They had the means to build the retreat and did so. Ridiculous ideas have sprouted from the urban legend about Nazis, such as: that it was to be Hitler's retreat, that the residents would emerge to repopulate a devastated country, that 50 people were arrested there right after Pearl Harbor, including Schmidt with his shortwave radio. I know these stories to be false, and there is no factual evidence to support them. I was there.

My oldest brother Dale served in the US military as General Patton's driver in Europe, my brother Robin served in the militarized merchant marine in the Pacific, and my father Norman worked with Douglas Aircraft during the war testing fighter planes. Our family served the United States well during World War II, and I am unhappy to hear tales of Nazis associated with our family.

My parents and the rest of the Stevens family moved to Ramona in July 1945. My mother never returned to the ranch. My father, myself, and my brother Robin returned from time to time to help maintain the property until it was sold to Huntington Hartford in 1949.

To my best knowledge and belief, the foregoing statements are true.
(signed)
Carlile R. Stevens

=.-

AFFIDAVIT – Robin Stevens
In connection with the history of Murphy Ranch in Rustic Canyon in Los Angeles, California, and the Stevens family that built it and lived there, I am furnishing the following information:

My name is Robin Campbell Stevens, the son of Norman F. and Winona Stevens (not Stephens). I lived at Murphy Ranch during the Second World

The True Story of Murphy Ranch

War, from November 25, 1942, through July 1945, except when I was away at school. When I moved there the residents were: Norman Stevens, Winona Stevens, my sister Theanne Stevens, brothers Dale and Carlile Stevens, Josephine Spotts, Ilsa Reynolds, Conrad Anderson, and Florence Kamp. Hired hands came and went.

Contrary to any urban legends about Nazis and Murphy Ranch, the entire time I was there I never saw anything related to Nazis or National Socialism. There were no guards, guard dogs, marches, gatherings, or Nazi insignias. There was no one speaking German, and there was no discussion of Nazis beyond what would be normal during World War II. There was no one named Schmidt there or ever discussed. There was more concern about the Japanese, who could attack the West Coast, than the Germans.

Conrad Anderson, who was a spiritual healer, lived in his own separate house and was already living there when we moved in. All the rest of us lived in a building of about 3000 square feet, with 7 bedrooms, other rooms, and a 4-car garage. This is labeled "servant's quarters" on the architectural drawings, and was the main building on the property, with the intention that more would be built.

Approximately $900,000 was spent to build out Murphy Ranch from 1932 through 1942. My mother, Winona, provided the money, which came from my grandfather Arthur Bassett, who had made a fortune developing the round nail in Chicago. The property was purchased from Jessie Murphy, who my parents and sister met with a number of times. The ranch was intended to be entirely self-sufficient. Only a phone line connected it to the outside world; the power came from generators and the water from wells.

My parents were strongly influenced by Conrad Anderson, who had healed me when I was very young and close to death when doctors and others had been unable to help. Anderson ran Murphy Ranch. Josephine Spotts and Ilsa Reynolds were wealthy followers of his who had given him their money. My parents were fascinated by his healing powers and predictions about the war and wanted to be safe whatever the outcome was. Anderson convinced them that they would be safe if they built their self-sufficient retreat. They had the means to build the retreat and did so. Ridiculous ideas have sprouted from the urban legend about Nazis, such as: that it was to be Hitler's retreat, that the residents would emerge to repopulate a devastated country, that 50 people were arrested there right after Pearl Harbor, including Schmidt with his shortwave radio. I know these stories to be false, and there is no factual evidence to support them. I was there.

My oldest brother Dale served in the US military as General Patton's driver in Europe, and my father Norman worked with Douglas Aircraft during the war testing fighter planes. I served in the militarized Merchant Marine in the Pacific and was among the first Americans to land in Japan, 7 days after the surrender. I served in the Army Reserve for many years after the war, as did my brothers. Our family served the United States well during World War II, and I am unhappy to hear tales of Nazis associated with our family.

My parents and the rest of the Stevens family moved to Ramona in July 1945. My mother never returned to the ranch and died in 1954. My father, myself, and my brother Carlile returned from time to time to help maintain the property until it was sold to Huntington Hartford in 1949.

To my best knowledge and belief, the foregoing statements are true.
(signed)
Robin Campbell Stevens

ABOUT THE AUTHOR

Stanton Stevens is a husband and father, retired from his long IT career. He lectures on the Esoteric Philosophy his grandfather introduced him to. His next project is a book based on his talks covering topics such as the Soul, the great truths and great lies, death, money and spirituality, esoteric Christianity, esoteric science, the next kingdom beyond human, esoteric relationships, etc.